# CLASS STRUCTURE
# IN THE SOCIAL CONSCIOUSNESS

342-6
57

**International Library of Sociology**

Founded by Karl Mannheim

Editor: John Rex, University of Aston in Birmingham

Arbor Scientiae
Arbor Vitae

A catalogue of the books available in the **International Library of Sociology** and other series of Social Science books published by Routledge & Kegan Paul will be found at the end of this volume.

# CLASS STRUCTURE
# IN THE
# SOCIAL CONSCIOUSNESS

by

STANISLAW OSSOWSKI

translated from the Polish by

SHEILA PATTERSON

ROUTLEDGE & KEGAN PAUL

LONDON, BOSTON AND HENLEY

Translated from the Polish
STRUKTURA KLASOWA W SPOLECZNEJ ŚWIADOMOŚCI

First published in Great Britain in 1963
by Routledge and Kegan Paul Ltd.
39 Store Street
London WC1E 7DD,
Broadway House, Newtown Road
Henley-on-Thames
Oxon RG9 1EN and
9 Park Street
Boston, Mass. 02108, USA

Printed in Great Britain by
Caledonian Graphics
Cumbernauld, Scotland

Reprinted in 1967, 1969 & 1973
Reprinted and first published
as a paperback in 1979

ISBN   0   7100   0532   6

# CONTENTS

v

# PREFACE

Nearly five years have passed since this book was originally published in the Polish language. Its appearance in print was in a certain sense linked with the events of October 1956 in Poland, for these made it possible to publish the work on which I had been engaged for several years without hope of publication. The book went to press in the post-October period of enthusiasm and hope, and this emotional climate was reflected in its final touches.

Since 1957 a number of sociological enquiries have been carried out in Poland; they include enquiries into social attitudes towards the problems of egalitarianism, the relationship to socialism in various social milieux in our country and the ways in which socialism is conceived. The speed of social change in the world means that we often look back at events that happened only a few years before from a historical perspective. None the less it seems to me that the events of the intervening period have produced nothing that would necessitate any changes in the contents of this book, the subject matter of which consists of problems that are not confined to a single country, system or period.

The book of course reflects in various respects the conditions prevailing in the country in which it was written. Sometimes this affects the manner in which problems are presented. At other times it may emerge in certain reflexions or allusions or in the citing of instances which are of particular importance for the situation that prevailed in Poland before October 1956. For instance, the reference in the introduction to the coincidence between the entirely independent views of Prus and Engels, which an English-speaking reader may regard as unessential, was in reaction to the view propagated in Eastern Europe about the absolute contrast between the Marxist classics and positivistic 'bourgeois' thought.

For a considerable period Poland has lain at a crossroads of various trends of thought. She possesses old-established sociological traditions linked with the names of Joachim Lelewel

PREFACE

(1786–1861), Ludwik Gumplowicz (1838–1909), Ludwik Krzywicki (1859–1941), Edward Abramowski (1869–1918), Stefan
Czarnowski (1879–1937), and Florian Znaniecki (1882–1958).
At the turn of this Century some Polish sociologists (including
Krzywicki, Abramowski and Kelles-Krauz) were not only
academic sociologists but revolutionary thinkers who participated
in the revolutionary movement. The first Polish translations of
Marx's works appeared as early as the 1860's. The Polish Sociological Institute, which was founded by Znaniecki in 1921,
carried on underground academic work all through the Nazi
occupation of 1939–1944. After the Second World War Poland
was an area in which the sociological concepts of Western Europe
and the United States clashed with the Marxist method of interpreting phenomena according to the line laid down by the Party.
This clash between differing ways of thinking stimulated the
raising of some special questions which are discussed in various
chapters of this book, and encouraged the search for problems of
world-wide importance, despite the view expressed in official
circles about the distinctness of the social problems found in the
so-called 'Western World' and those of the socialist countries.

The English translation of this study is a break-through of the
language barrier to a wider readership. It is particularly important
to me because of the subject-matter of this book.

The translation was not an easy task, mainly because of the
difficulties arising out of the different connotations of the Polish
conceptual apparatus and of the English one. I should like to express my deep gratitude to Mrs. Sheila Patterson for her work,
performed with such care and competence. I should also like to
record my sincerest thanks to Dr. Zbigniew Jordan for his co-
operation with Mrs. Patterson in checking the draft translation
and for his valuable advice on a number of points for the final
English version of this work.

STANISLAW OSSOWSKI

*June 1962.*

# Chapter I

# INTRODUCTION

*Social Problems in the Light of New Experience*

THE CONDITIONS in which the modern capitalist economy developed gave birth to classical economics, bourgeois sociology and historical materialism. Bourgeois sociology and economics assumed that the capitalist system would be lasting. Historical materialism regarded the capitalist economy as a passing stage in historical development but Marx devoted nearly his whole life to the study of capitalist society. In their formulation of general laws both he and Engels availed themselves of the same direct experiences as did sociologists like Spencer and the founders of classical economics. All these theories treat society as an aggregate of individuals which in general observes certain rules of the game, these rules being expressed in legal codes, constitutions and above all in conventions regulating economic relations, particularly those on the free market; an aggregate of individuals each of whom on the whole follows his own decisions, although these decisions are determined by certain laws of nature. Similarly determined by general laws are the overall results of the interaction of these countless individual decisions. This is, *inter alia*, the way in which the Marxian laws of historical development function.

The controversies between Marxism and liberal sociology assumed their sharpest form when they were considered against the background of certain assumptions which were common to both sides. This will emerge more distinctly in later chapters. Meanwhile it will suffice to compare the observations made by Engels in his study of Ludwig Feuerbach in 1888 with the reflections of the Polish novelist, Boleslaw Prus, on the laws governing the development of Paris. Prus was the author of *The Doll*, which popularized in Poland the positivist conception of society held by bourgeois liberals. This novel was serialized in the Warsaw *Kurier Codzienny* (*Daily Courier*) in the years 1887–9 – and thus appeared at the same time as *Ludwig Feuerbach*:

'So the work of the millions of people who make such a loud clamour about their free will brings the same results as that of the bees constructing their orderly honey-combs, of the ants raising their conical hills or of the chemical combinations that form themselves into regular crystals.' (Prus, *The Doll* (*Lalka*) Vol II. Chapter VIII).

'Thus the conflicts of innumerable individual wills and individual actions in the domain of history produce a state of affairs entirely analogous to that prevailing in the realm of unconscious nature.'[1]

'Thus there is no chance in society, but an inflexible law, which as if in irony at human haughtiness, reveals itself so distinctly in the life of that most capricious nation, the French.' (Prus, *op. cit.*)

'But where on the surface accident holds sway, there actually it is always governed by inner, hidden laws and it is only a matter of discovering these laws. Men make their own history . . . in that each person follows his own consciously desired end, and it is precisely the resultant of these many wills operating in different directions and of their manifold effects upon the outer world that constitutes history.' (ME, Vol. II, p. 354).

The events of recent decades have immensely enriched the range of knowledge available to the student of social life. When the conceptual system and problems of bourgeois sociology were being formulated, when the ideas of Marx and Engels were being developed into a great and cohesive doctrine, the social consequences of the second technical revolution (electricity and the internal combustion engine) which were to transform the social life of the twentieth century were not yet known. And the prospects revealed to us by the release of atomic energy, prospects of a new civilization or of universal destruction, were at that time

[1] Karl Marx and Frederick Engels, *Selected Works in Two Volumes*, Moscow, Foreign Languages Publishing House, 1951 (quoted hereafter in abbreviation 'ME') Vol. II, p. 354. The quotation comes from F. Engels, *Ludwig Feuerbach and the End of Classical German Philosophy*.

not even a subject for writers of science fantasy. That age had no knowledge of the extermination camps which were to be organized by representatives of the nation which played a leading part in the annals of European civilization. A vision of the liberation of colonial peoples in a period when the division of the world between the European powers was reaching its end could at the best seem like a naive dream of utopian-minded humanitarians. A social system based on the nationalization of the means of production was also unknown. No one could yet have had any experience of the kind of planning which was over a great part of the globe to embrace in a centralized system almost the entire economy, including the production of the so-called 'cultural values', and to take over the direction of the labour force, the large-scale distribution of privileges and discriminations and the conscious shaping of the social structure.

In the era in which bourgeois society was dominated by liberal ideology and the radical variety of socialism was a current of liberation everywhere it could make itself felt, these aspects of modern techniques went unnoticed. They only acquired significance for us after modern technological achievements gave to those who hold political authority not only the vast powers of control over nature, foretold by the nineteenth-century scientists, but also of control over man, individually and *en masse*.

Faced with these new experiences, it is hard to resist the impression that the conditions in which the theories of the nineteenth century originated have handicapped the further development of the social sciences. It is no easy thing to free oneself from the traditional manner of comprehending phenomena or stating problems in the sphere of human affairs, or to free oneself from the suggestive influences imposed by the framework of the traditional conceptual apparatus. It is no easy task even when the conservatism of theoretical thought is not overshadowed by a revolutionary programme of action and reinforced by the sanctions of the reigning ideology – as happens in countries where socialism has been victorious – or when this conservatism is not an expression of nostalgia for a vanished epoch, as is the case with the liberals of today. In the social sciences theoretical conceptions sometimes anticipate life, and become a guide for men of action. In periods of violent change, however, the theorist cannot keep pace with life. Reality then changes more rapidly than does reflective thought, which is left breathless by the rate of change at a time a deep breath is most needed. This would seem to be the case today.

This new stage of development, to use the Marxian phrase, imposes new social problems of the utmost importance, and demands new assumptions, new concepts and new methods. Moreover the fresh store of experiences, which are new in so many important respects, also inclines one to take a new look at the whole arsenal of facts amassed in the past.

In the history of learning it has often happened that scholars have overlooked certain phenomena although these were within the scope of their experience, and that these phenomena attracted notice only when analogous phenomena on a far larger scale struck the scholar's eye in a different situation. The events which incline us to regard our own time as the beginning of a new era are so large in scale, as far as the depth of the transformation and the importance of their practical consequences is concerned, and their range is so great, in the sense of the number of people and the extent of the earth's surface affected, that an analysis of these events can also change our view of the past. Certain phenomena and certain relationships in past eras could have escaped our notice, although they were significant in social life even then; they could have escaped notice because they were screened by facts and relationships which were more characteristic of the epoch. They could also have been regarded as accidental and devoid of any real significance, and thus have been consciously omitted in broad generalizations so as to give a more distinct picture of the events considered.

But an analysis of phenomena that are significant for the world of today can also incline us to restrict the generality of our basic sociological assumptions or to try to achieve a higher degree of generalization by means of some synthesis of views based on different experiences.

Such is the case, for instance, with the fertile and revealing nineteenth-century theory concerning the antagonism between social classes as the driving force of history – if we choose to make use of experiences which the founders of historical materialism did not live to see. The conflicts between organizations, propagating class ideology on behalf of the same class, particularly after 1917, or the processes which in mono-party systems came to be called 'the estrangement of the party from the masses' showed that it is just as much possible to use class interests as a mask for party interests as it is to disguise class interests by means of universal or national slogans in organizations whose ideology is allegedly not class-bound. These experiences and others like them have taught us that the relationship between social classes and large social organizations is more complicated than was assumed in the Marxian view of the dynamics of history; and that the antagonisms in which we may seek the driving force of history are at work on more than one level.

When the comparative material is extended to include phenomena that appears unprecedented in certain respects which we regard as important, one can anticipate that the conceptual categories which sufficed for earlier generalizations will appear unsuitable or inadequate. Changes in social reality may therefore involve changes in the conceptual apparatus, not only to enable one to describe the new phenomena but also to formulate general hypotheses which will take the old and the new experiences into account.

The consequence of such reflexions is to incline us, when observing the phenomena which are actually passing in front of our eyes, to examine problems whose application is not confined to one era: i.e. the basic problems of social structure and the dynamics of social life. In speaking here of social structure, I am concerned with the categories of social relations and roles which are involved in the history of the ideologies built around such rallying-cries as freedom, equality, and social justice, and in the history of the domination of social groups or organizations and of the struggle against various forms of oppression within the framework of the whole society.

There are a number of old problems which one would now like to re-examine or at least restate, in the perhaps illusory hope that this would stimulate further investigation and would in some way prove of use in the search for solutions to those burning social problems which plague us at present.

They include systems of interdependent human relations and the privileges of ownership, spontaneous and organized relations within a social structure, the types of ideological divisions involved in the great social conflicts and the functions of social ideologies in the shaping of social life.

Such was my original intention when I began this study in the winter of 1951. In undertaking to carry out an analysis of basic human relationships of the most general nature, it was difficult not to take an interest in the ways in which people belonging to different collectivities see the structure of their own society. For reasons which I shall give shortly, I decided to investigate the main ways of describing social structure and to precede any direct discussion of social structure with a scrutiny of the forms which the system of human relationships assumes in the social consciousness under differing conditions.

These enquiries resulted in a separate study to which I gave the title *Class Structure in the Social Consciousness* and which ultimately grew into the present book. I do not think there is any need to fear the danger of reification which encumbers the term 'social consciousness' if I explain now how I propose to use it. I shall be using the term as an abbreviation to refer to the ideas that characterize certain milieux, for the concepts, images, beliefs and evaluations that are more or less common to people of a certain social environment and which are reinforced in the consciousness of particular individuals by mutual suggestion and by the conviction that they are shared by other people in the same group. This latter consideration means that the expression 'in the social consciousness' has a richer connotation than the expression 'in the consciousness of the individuals who belong to a particular group'.

The way in which the social structure appears to those who are part of it is important for various reasons:

(*a*) A view of the social structure which is widely held is an element in the social situation, and thus exerts an influence on the nature of human relations.

(*b*) A way of perceiving the social structure which is more or less generally accepted in certain classes or milieux allows us to conclude which elements in the system of relationships seem particularly important in the eyes of their members. It is through such environmental images of human relationships that we can reach the pertinent problems.

(*c*) If we accept that the establishment of certain analogies in the manner of perceiving social structure in different types of society and in different historical epochs can throw light on the basic characteristics of social structure in class systems, then we may also agree that a comparison of mentally opposed or widely differing ways of perceiving the same social structure can make it easier to achieve a thorough insight into the system of human relationships. Different images of the same structure do not merely express different propensities: they represent a stock of different experiences and observations resulting from differing practical interests. Moreover our knowledge about social structure is deepened when we endeavour to explain the different ways of perceiving social structure and to find the causes of these differences. This applies not only to the modes of perception peculiar to certain environments but also to the mutually exclusive conceptions of the sociologists. For instance, it is highly instructive to compare the Marxian theory of social classes with those of American sociologists in this respect. This question is a complicated one since it involves not only different social propensities and interests but also differences in the data used.

(d) Finally, images of social structure, especially those which are socially determined, are important for us because they directly condition social ideologies and social programmes. Thus a review of conceptions of social structure in the social consciousness would constitute a sort of prolegomena both to investigations of systems of human relationships and to comparative studies of the function of social ideologies.

## Metaphors and Conceptual Content

One of the tasks that we face in undertaking an analysis of the social conceptions that are characteristic of a particular social environment is to penetrate to the essential meaning of metaphors that are in common use. In considering the general problems of social structure and the types and transformations of social systems, or in investigations of the social structure in particular countries, we generally make considerable use of terms with a spatial connotation. 'Social stratification', 'social strata', 'upper and lower classes', 'upper-middle and lower-middle classes', 'social distance', the 'boundaries of social groups' and the 'rigidity' of these boundaries, the 'contiguity and isolation of groups', the movement of individuals from group to group 'in a vertical or horizontal direction' – all these terms refer to spatial relations. And we have become so accustomed to their metaphorical meaning when we are discussing social structure that we are not generally even conscious of their metaphorical character.

In the Marxian theory of social structure and in Marxist literature there are, for reasons which will be given later, fewer terms drawn from spatial relations; but the language which the Marxists use to describe social structure and its changes is nevertheless rich in metaphors. The writing of Marx, Engels and the founders of the Soviet state are officially held to combine the highest political and the highest scientific authority, and have played an immense political role in the past and now. In consequence, Marxist circles have developed an unusual technique of employing vague metaphors and terms; the practical value of this technique has been successfully tested over a long period.

'Mankind always sets itself only such tasks as it can solve.'[1] 'Classes are large groups of people which differ from each other by the place they occupy in a historically determined system of social production.'[2] 'The superstructure is created by the basis precisely in order to serve it, to actively help it to take shape and consolidate itself, to actively fight for the elimination of the old moribund basis.'[3]

These are some examples of statements which have been cited hundreds of times in many different languages.

Metaphorical expressions whose meaning has never been clarified in such a way as to make it possible to regard them as new terms cease through common use to impress one as metaphors. Through such common use their new meaning becomes the current meaning, emancipated to a certain extent from the original meaning. None the less a legacy of the metaphors is perceived in pictorial associations with an intuitive appeal. Owing to this intuition on the one hand and routine on the other, one usually does not feel a need to ask how one should understand 'place in the system of production' or 'the creation of a superstructure by the base', particularly where such expressions are supported by quotations from works of the highest political authority and meet the criterion of practical utility.

Questions about the meaning of phrases or terms in the social sciences can be dangerous for the routine ways of thinking if the inquirer is not satisfied with an exemplification. This is not merely

[1] Karl Marx: *Preface to the Critique of Political Economy* (ME, Vol. I, p. 329).

[2] V. I. Lenin: 'A Great Beginning' (see *The Essentials of Lenin*, London, Lawrence and Wishart, 1947; Vol. II, p. 492).

[3] J. Stalin: *Marxism and Problems of Linguistics*, Moscow, Foreign Languages Publishing House, 1954; pp. 9–10.

because such questioning can disturb established verbal usage but also because it can reveal new problems which were formerly screened by ambiguous terminology and conceptual condensations. This sometimes happens during the analysis of a segment of reality, when we endeavour to replace metaphors, verbal associations, and an intuitive understanding of the matter by formulating the conceptual content of the respective terms. The aim here is not to eliminate all metaphors from the language of the social sciences but to achieve the conceptual clarification that is essential for the enquiry that has been undertaken.

## The Concept of Structure

We have already spoken of the spatial character of some of the metaphors that refer to social structure. The term 'structure' is in fact also borrowed from the spatial world; and the concepts of social structure and class structure play so great a role in this enquiry that I must devote a little time to them now.

By 'structure' in its literal meaning we understand a spatial arrangement of elements, in which we regard spatial relations as being correlated with some system of relationships between these elements or between particular parts and the whole. The structure of a building is described in terms of the arrangement of elements fulfilling specific functions in relation to the building's purpose: e.g. the pillars and arches support the vault while the roof shields the interior from rain. The structure of a living organism is the arrangement of tissues and organs which fulfil specific functions in the life process. The structure of a painting is a two-dimensional arrangement of patches of colour, each of which by means of its quality and shape exerts an influence on one's interpretation of the remaining patches and on the effect produced by the painting as a whole.

In a metaphorical sense, structure is a system of figuratively interpreted distances and relations of one sort or another. In this sense one can for instance speak of the structure of the patriarchal family; here a closer kinship links the children with their father than with their mother, and the bond linking the father with his first-born son is stronger than that between him and his other children. In this sense, too, we contrast this patriarchal structure with the structure of the Melanesian family, where the husband is linked by close bonds to his wife but has no institutionalized relationship with his own children and where the children's closest kinsman is their maternal uncle, while their father is most closely linked with his sister's children.

The structure of society can be interpreted in a literal, spatial sense. This happens when we study the spatial arrangement of individuals and groups with regard to the social relations which arise between them. By the spatial arrangement of individuals and groups, I am thinking here of the size, distribution and spatial form of settlements, the density of population in particular sectors of a territory, the lines of communication and so on. The problems of the spatial structure of society, so understood, where the terms (such as 'distance', 'isolation', 'boundary') that refer to spatial relations retain their original meaning, are also included in the problems of the social sciences. One does not however usually apply the term 'social structure' to the structure of society in this literal, spatial sense. French scholars have evolved a special discipline for this under the name of 'social morphology', while the Americans group these problems within the framework of 'social ecology', which allows room for 'ecological structure'.

The adjective 'social' deprives the term 'structure' of its spatial connotation, just as is the case with such terms as 'distance' or 'mobility'. 'Social distance' does not denote spatial distance, while 'social mobility' does not refer to mobility in space.

In contrast to such 'microstructures' as a family structure, which is a system of relationships between particular individuals, we speak of 'social structure' only when we are treating whole groups or categories of individuals, but not particular individuals, as elements of the system. The concept of social structure is wider than that of class structure, since the groups which we regard as elements in social structure need not be social classes. They could for instance be age categories (e.g. children, young people, grown men, elders) which we are investigating to ascertain the institutionalized relationships and division of functions between them, or the different rights and obligations attached to each age-category. They could also be ethnic groups: in a plural society of this kind we could be interested in the hierarchy of prestige in which the different ethnic groups are arranged and in the extent of the social distances between the respective groups; these are the subject of frequent investigation in the United States. Moreover, in speaking of social structure, we can take such organized groups such as political parties or bureaucratic and church hierarchies into consideration.

I therefore conceive of social structure as a system of human relationships, distances and hierarchies in both an organized and an unorganized form. Class structure I regard as a particular and especially important aspect of social structure. In speaking of human relationships I have in mind both the relationships that result from power relations and those that result from the division of functions.

It is perhaps worth stressing that, in referring to human societies, the term 'structure' is sometimes used in situations where it does not refer either to relations of dependence or to social distance. One speaks, for example, of demographic, occupational, denominational or racial structure, when one is simply referring to the composition of the population in a particular respect. If it is necessary to refer to this sort of situation during the course of my enquiry, I shall speak of the 'composition' of the population and not of its 'structure'.

The concept of social class requires analysis. I shall however defer this until I have considered a number of conceptions of class structure and several other issues, such as the two ways of conceiving of a classless society or the interpretation of the distinctness of class boundaries. Once in possession of the varied material made available by the discussion of these issues, it will be easier to formulate the problems arising out of the ambiguity of the term 'social class' and to indicate the common conceptual content in various statements concerning social class.

For the present, I should like to emphasize that in the chapters that precede the analysis of the concept of class I shall be using the term 'social class' in the most general sense, and also in the sense which is most important in historical perspective because of the lasting interest of the questions involved. I shall be using it in the sense in which, when speaking for instance of the 'class struggle', one includes in this term slave revolts and peasant wars, struggles between patricians and plebeians in ancient Rome, or between the nobility and the bourgeoisie in more recent revolutions, as well as the struggle between capitalists and the proletariat and even between medium and large-scale capitalists.

# INTRODUCTION

## Historical Material and General Conclusions

As I have already stated, this enquiry has a twofold character and has set itself a two-fold task. It has been my endeavour to consider in the light of recent experiences certain problems which have maintained their importance and relevance for centuries in class societies. I have at the same time attempted to make use of the results of these comparative investigations in order to grasp and emphasize the historical transformations of the nineteenth and twentieth centuries.

To carry out an adequately comprehensive systematization of the basic ways of interpreting class structure it was necessary to make use of materials taken from different epochs and different systems. Thus Aristotle may turn up as a neighbour of American sociological writers, and Winstanley and the Church Fathers next to Karl Marx.

This study does not however give a historical survey of viewpoints, concepts and ideas. The task here was not to write a history of conceptions of class structure within the limits defined by the choice of material, but to systematize these conceptions. Nor was it the task of this study to inquire into the degree to which various conceptions were generally accepted at different periods, although I have as far as possible tried to use material that is representative of particular social environments. In selecting material I paid special attention to those writings which played an important part in the history of social thought and social movements. This was because I intended the systematization at which I was aiming to be a systematization of those views of class structure which have been important as social facts.

The selection of material from several thousand years of recorded history to serve as a basis for sociological generalizations must always be more or less fortuitous. Nor can the criterion mentioned above prevent this at all. Some general statements do not, however, require a systematic selection of material or an investigation of the representative nature of the data. We are entitled to draw certain negative conclusions even from fragmentary data – such as the statement that the particular ways of conceiving the social structure which are the subject-matter of this study are not correlated with particular 'formations' of class-societies, or that dichotomic ways of perceiving class structure are not of significance for the under-privileged classes only. Such conclusions require only one instance, so long as this is thoroughly investigated in its historical contest.

Sometimes the material at hand allowed me to formulate hypotheses which needed to be tested on material to be found elsewhere. I am thinking here of conclusions concerned with the circumstances which favour the formation and increasing acceptance of a particular way of perceiving the social order, (as for instance in the last part of Chapter II or the last paragraph of Chapter IV).

More general conclusions and explanations, which could fall within the domain of the sociology of knowledge, such as the statements dealing with the motives behind terminological disputes which are to be found in Chapter XI or the observations about the relations between the typology of interpretations of social structure and the typology of social structures which are made in Chapter XII, spring from a wider experience than that based on the materials to which direct reference is made here.

As I have already mentioned, I have tried as far as was possible to select material that has played a significant and representative role in the history of social thought and social movements, in so far as European culture is concerned. Only exceptionally and in a few cases did I look to Asian cultures for examples, and even in the case of the Old Testament I usually examined it through the eyes and reactions of Christian readers of the Bible. Thus, although I have set no limits of space or time to my examination of conceptions of class structure, this enquiry may therefore be regarded as a study of class-societies in the realm of European culture.

This does not mean that I consider that a historical sweep which ranges from Aristotle and the Church Fathers to the contemporary American and Soviet writers is not wide enough to permit the formulation of broader hypotheses, hypotheses which would be more than historical generalizations set within the framework of European culture. Undoubtedly the distance between early mediaeval society and contemporary French or Norwegian society is greater, seen from the viewpoint of my particular interests, than is the distance between European mediaeval society and Chinese or Indian mediaeval society. This gives rise to a certain duality in the treatment of my general conclusions, including the classification of class structures given in Chapter X. This I should like to regard as an attempt to systematize the ways of interpreting class structure in general and not only the ways of interpreting class structure found in European culture. This is not an exceptional case. All the materials which the sociologist can use are contained within some limits of time and space, and the question of the criteria for differentiating historical generalizations from sociological generalizations is by no means a simple one.

The greater part of the material which is used here consists of the works and statements of various writers. Some of these present the views current in a particular environment, as in the case of contemporary American sociological field-workers. But we shall also be using, and in fact devoting most space to an analysis of the personal conceptions of thinkers and theorists. This may give rise to doubts whether I have not deviated from my objective, and whether I am really dealing throughout with conceptions of social structure in the social consciousness.

In my view, the typological tasks which have emerged in these chapters do not conflict with the subject indicated in the title of this study, because I do not go beyond those ways of perceiving social structure which have played an important role in social life. Seen from this angle the Gospels and the Koran, the works of Aristotle and Aquinas, of Adam Smith and Marx, the homilies of St. John Chrysostom, the letters of Babeuf, Saint-Simon's articles, Spencer's studies and the writings of Lenin do not simply represent those who wrote them. In this enquiry we are concerned with these writings because of the cultural processes of which they were a part, i.e. because of their connexion with the environments which produced them and were influenced by them later.

## Outline of this Study

The aim of this preliminary chapter was to introduce readers to the problems to be investigated, to explain the way in which the study originated and to give at least a provisional interpretation of certain terms. The remainder of the book falls into two parts.

The chapters in Part I are concerned with various interpretations of social structure. The first three chapters have as their subject the basic ways of perceiving the systems of social relations in a class-society, as found in different social systems and in different epochs. The next three chapters (V, VI, and VII) deal with the conceptions that have arisen in nineteenth- and twentieth-century societies.

In Part II I shall endeavour to make a synthetic use of the results arrived at in Part I.

Chapters VIII and IX are devoted to a consideration of the concept of class and also to the question of the relations between the paradigm of a social class and the definitions of class given by the theoretical writers of the nineteenth and twentieth centuries. Chapter X contains a systematization of the results of the first part of the book and an attempt to classify various types of interpretation of class structure; its starting point is provided by the examination of the concept of social class carried out in Chapter IX. Chapter XI develops the discussion of certain problems which emerged in the examination of the concept of class in the wider context of the 'sociology of knowledge'. Finally, in Chapter XII the problem of the relations between the ways of interpreting class structure and the types of class structure are discussed; here I have endeavoured to draw certain conclusions from an examination of the persistence of ways of conceiving of human relationships in the light of the social changes of recent centuries. The final problem discussed is that of historical comparisons in association with the fate of revolutionary ideologies.

# Part I

FROM BIBLICAL LEGENDS TO
CONTEMPORARY SOCIOLOGY

# Chapter II

## DICHOTOMIC CONCEPTIONS OF CLASS STRUCTURE – ONE GROUP SET OVER ANOTHER

IN THE PRECEDING chapter I referred to the spatial metaphors of the vertical stratification of social classes, which represents a society as an aggregate of people, of whom some are above and others below. This is one of those images that retain their vitality over the centuries and which – so the history of differing cultures would seem to show – spontaneously impose themselves upon the imagination.

This universal image, which we may treat as the reflection of the class system in the social consciousness, is backed in cultural history by the authority of old religious myths such as the Biblical story of Ham or the Hindu myth explaining the genesis of the four fundamental castes.

It was the sin of Ham, whose offspring were cursed by the enraged Noah and condemned to eternal bondage in the service of the descendants of Ham's worthy brethren, that was cited by St. Augustine when he wished to prove that slavery, though contrary to human nature, is justified by the sins which have warped man's nature. The sin and the curse of Ham were also cited by those who defended serfdom in the Middle Ages and by the American ministers of religion who in the first half of the nineteenth century used Biblical arguments to combat the abolitionists whose aim was to liberate the Negro slaves. In the Veda scriptures, the vertical system of social strata was given an anatomical illustration. It was said that the Brahmins sprang from the lips of Brahma, the Kshatriya from his shoulders, the Vaishya from his thighs and the Shudra from his feet. According to the Koran, social stratification originates directly from the will of Allah:

'We have exalted some of them above others in degrees, that some of them may take others in subjection . . .'[1]

The same thought was expressed in a mediaeval English verse, inspired by the philosophy of the established Church:

> "The rich man at his castle,
> The poor man at his gate.
> God made them high or lowly
> And ordered their estate."

The etymology of the Polish word *bogaty*, meaning 'rich' (*Bóg* means 'God'), probably indicates a similar view.

The concept of social structure as a 'vertical' order has taken various concrete forms. When we turn to folk-lore or to the heritage left behind by social and political leaders – from the prophetic writings of Judea and Israel to the revolutionary manifestos of the nineteenth and twentieth century – we are forced to conclude that the most popular, or at all events the most socially significant view of social stratification is the dichotomic one which perceives societies as divided into two main groups, consisting of those who are at the top and those who are at the bottom. The deep significance of this view arises out of the fact that it is an *idée force* in its function in social movements.

This most simple form of stratification also finds support in religious myths. The Levellers, that extreme radical wing in the Cromwellian revolution, took the ideal of universal equality as their war-cry, and used the Book of Genesis to illustrate their image of English social structure at that time. Cain against Abel, Ishmael against Isaac (*sic*), Esau against Jacob – in their view these three represented those who had illegally seized the power and the land and had turned their brothers into servants.[2] As can be seen, the interpretation of Biblical myths given by these worshippers of Holy Writ does not take much note of the Biblical text.

---

[1] *Koran*, Ch. XLIII v. 32, English translation by Maulvi Muhammad Ali, Ahmadiyya Anjuman-i-ishàat Islam, Lahore, 1920.

[2] G. Winstanley, "The True Levellers Standard Advanced (1649)" in *The Works of G. Winstanley*, New York 1941, pp 252–3.

It is simply a case of using every example in which two brothers, the one good, the other bad, can be made to represent the dichotomic division of society between oppressers and oppressed.

With the Levellers, the dichotomy was mainly concerned with the question of land ownership. Winstanley, their leading writer, traced the origin of the split in English society to the Norman Conquest, which enslaved the English people, or 'English Israelites', as he called them in another reference to the Old Testament.[1]

In his defence of the oppressed class, Winstanley made no reference to the myth of Ham, which the representatives of the ruling class had used so readily. For the Levellers, the forefather of the privileged oppressers was Cain, and not those Biblical characters who rejoiced in the Divine grace. But the relationship between Cain and Abel affords an interesting subject for a sociologist. For the myth of the first fratricide has been interpreted in other ways. We read in a collection of legends of the Cracow region compiled by Oskar Kolberg:[2]

'The angel gave orders to Cain that for his whole life he should work not only for his own children but also for the descendants of Abel, whom he permitted to live on earth, doing nothing but faring well. So from Abel come the kings and the lords, but from Cain the serfs working for the benefit of the masters. . . . What good did Cain do? He created serfdom; now the poor must work for the rich men.'

For the Levellers, therefore, Cain symbolized those who owned the land; but amongst the Polish serfs he became the forefather of their own group. Thus the same dichotomy can acquire one symbolic meaning amongst those who are prepared for active revolt, and quite another amongst those who accept their lot with resignation and acquiesce in the ideology imposed on them by the privileged class above. For instance, Jakub Szela, the leader of a peasant revolt against the landlords in Southern Poland in 1846, was fond of referring to the Scriptures, but he would not have identified the descendants of Abel with the Polish landlords.

The voice of revolt can however reach further than it did with the Levellers. It can attack the scale of values which each of the contending sides endeavours to achieve for its own cause. Then

[1] *Ibid.* p. 259.
[2] A Polish ethnographer of the first half of the nineteenth century.

Cain may again become the symbol of the oppressed, from whom the privileged class has reft not only their worldly goods but also their dignity and good name, and at the same time secured a monopoly of the grace of the Almighty, who sides with the powerful. This was the manner in which Baudelaire conceived the opposition of the 'race of Cain' and the 'race of Abel' in his ironic poem *Abel et Caïn*. Instead of rejecting the theme that the oppressed are an accursed race, the poet addressed himself to the accursed:

> 'Race de Caïn au ciel monte
> Et sur la terre jette Dieu!'

This is yet a third version of the class-interpretation of the myth of the blessed and the accursed brother.

At the beginning of this chapter mention was made of the Veda myth of the origin of the four main castes. This myth also permits the social structure to be conceived in a dichotomic scheme. And here again, we find differing interpretations of the anatomical dichotomy corresponding to the inclinations of the different classes. In one interpretation, it is the navel of Brahma that divides the two higher castes (*Aria Varna*) from the two lower castes (*Dasa Varna*). In a second, the main line of division runs below Brahma's thighs. The Shudra are said to have sprung from the deity's feet as a sign that their place is at the feet of the other three castes as their servants.

In Christianity, the dichotomic image of the social structure was transposed into the next world, the spatial metaphor finding a literal application in the topography of heaven and hell. While the redeemed rose up to heaven, the damned fell into the abyss. This transposition of the earthly dichotomy into the world beyond the grave found its most effective presentation not amongst the English Puritans, who in some respects regarded social relationships in the next world as a continuation of the economic stratification here on earth, but rather at the dawn of Christianity. Both St. Luke and St. James visualized the next world as a reversal of relationships on earth:

'And he lifted up his eyes on his disciples, and said, Blessed be ye poor: for yours is the kingdom of God.' (Luke VI v. 20.)
'For it is easier for a camel to go through a needle's eye, than for a rich man to enter into the kingdom of God.' (Luke XVIII v. 25.)

'Let the brother of low degree rejoice in that he is exalted; But the rich in that he is made lower: because as the flower of the grass he shall pass away.

For the sun is no sooner risen with a burning heat, but it withereth the grass, and the flower thereof falleth, and the grace of the fashion of it perisheth; so also shall the rich man fade away in his ways.' (General Epistle of James, I v. 9–11.)

'Hearken, my beloved brethren, Hath not God chosen the poor of this world rich in faith, and heirs of the kingdom which he hath promised to them that love him?' (General Epistle of James, II v. 5.)

This sort of image is vividly illustrated in the parable of Lazarus and the rich man.[1]

## A Three-Fold Dichotomy

The metaphor of spatial polar division (between the top and the bottom) symbolises a relation which, if we discard the metaphor, can be interpreted and formulated in various ways. Amongst these differing formulations we find three basic aspects of that dichotomy, corresponding to the three categories of privileges enjoyed by the upper stratum: (1) the rulers and the ruled (or, to put it in a way closer to the sentiments of the ruled, those who give orders and those who must obey); (2) the rich and the poor; (3) those for whom others work and those who work.

The first relation is expressed in the term 'the ruling classes', while an alternative formulation for the second relation is 'the propertied classes' and 'the propertyless classes'. In opposing the 'exploiters' to the 'exploited' we are referring to the third relation only, but a moral evaluation is discernible in this last formulation. A moral evaluation is even more evident in such expressions as

[1] Luke XVI, 19–31. This sharp opposition between the world of the damned and the world of the redeemed has been of use in various situations. But apparently it did not meet every social need from the viewpoint of the Catholic Church, for the Church introduced a third intermediate sphere into the next world – Purgatory – for which there is no direct scriptural authority. This intermediate sphere is not, it is true, equivalent to the others and it is in a certain sense transitory, since its duration is limited, in contrast to the two main spheres, which are to be eternal. Before the Last Judgment, the inhabitants of Purgatory are to move to Heaven, in the same way as the members of the petit bourgeoisie, with only a few exceptions, are in the Communist Manifesto visualised as joining the proletarian mass before the final judgement day or earlier. It is this transitoriness of Purgatory that has allowed the Catholic Church to make use of a dichotomic or a structural scheme of the next world according to its needs. In this respect, it has afforded the Catholic Church greater possibilities than are available to the Protestant Churches.

'oppressors' and 'oppressed'. Here we have the moral aspects of the basic dichotomy, as they are seen from the viewpoint of those at the bottom. But when we disregard moral evaluations and ask in terms of which 'objective' categories a given relation between the upper and lower stratum is conceived, it will, I think, become clear that this relation is confined to the three basic ones mentioned above.

These formulations are not of course mutually exclusive nor are they interchangeable. For the most part, we see in them three different relations which characterise the polar division between the upper and lower strata in the same cases, but with one of the relations being treated as fundamental from the viewpoint of casual relationships: this fundamental relation is either the first relation (of ruler and ruled) or the second (of rich and poor). The third relation (of those for whom others work and those who work) usually appears as the effect of either the first or the second relation, or of the conjunction of both. People work for those who rule them *because* they are their rulers. They work for those who are rich *because* they are rich.[1] Depending on whether the first or the second relation is given precedence, the association of power with wealth permits a two-fold interpretation of a dichotomic social structure:

(*a*) The precedence of power is expressed in such a formula as this – those at the top are rich because they rule, "The possession of power is the source of riches," said Ibn Khaldun at the turn of the fourteenth century.[2]

*b*) Those at the top rule because they are rich – this is the formula

---

[1] Some decades before the French Revolution (probably in 1711), the manifold ways in which the 'haves' could wrong the 'have nots' were brought out emphatically by the parish priest Father J. Meslier in his *Testament*. Undoubtedly he looked at these matters through the eyes of his parishioners from Estrepigny: when he wrote of 'une si étrange et si odieuse disproportion entre les differens états et conditions des hommes, qui met, comme on le voit manifestement, toute l'autorité, tous les biens, tous les plaisirs, tous les contentements, toutes les richesses et même l'oisiveté du côté des grands, des riches et des nobles, et met du côté des pauvres peuples tout ce qu'il y a de pénible et de facheux, savoir la dépendance, les soins, la misère, les inquiétudes, toutes les peines et toutes les fatigues du travail; laquelle disproportion est d'autant plus injuste et odieuse, qu'elle les met dans une entière dépendance des nobles et des riches, et qu'elle les rend pour ainsi dire leurs esclaves, jusques-là qu'ils sont obligés de souffrir non seulement toutes leurs rebufades, leurs mépris et leurs injures, mais aussi leurs véxations, leurs injustices et leurs mauvais traitements'. (*Le Testament de Jean Meslier*, Amsterdam, 1864, Vol. II, p. 178).

[2] *Les Prolégomènes*, (French translation), Vol. II, Paris 1936, p. 339.

that gives precedence to wealth. This view meets the basic claim of the capitalist ideology, and is at the same time a conclusion drawn from the assumptions of historical materialism, at least in relation to capitalist society. During the first World War, Spengler contended with some justice that the meaning ascribed to class differences in England and Prussia was not identical, since the inhabitants of England envisaged the class structure as being based on the division between rich and poor, while for the Prussians the nation was divided above all into those who gave orders and those who obeyed.[1]

As for the third aspect of the dichotomy, I have said that the exploitation of the labour of others may, so far as causal relationships are concerned, be regarded as resulting from the relation of power or that of ownership. None the less, the division between those for whom others work and those who work becomes a fundamental relation in another way in the eyes of members of the under-privileged stratum and of those who defend the cause of the stratum. For it is this relation which most directly determines the working man's mode of life and which sets a specific on his regular day-to-day activities – whether he is engaged on productive labour for another's profit or provides personal services for a man who can afford to live without working. This relation is shown in daily muscular effort, unalleviated by any pleasurable images of its anticipated reward. Constant compulsory labour 'for somebody else's benefit' weighs heavily on a man's body and mind. No wonder therefore that those who have found themselves in this enforced situation see the division of the social strata from this particular viewpoint.

*Bees and Drones*

It is the relation between those who work and those who do not, rather than the relationships of ownership or power, that is most clearly sounded in the rebellious question which rang throughout Europe in various versions in the fourteenth century.

> 'When Adam delved and Eve span,
> Who was then a gentleman?[2]

[1] O. Spengler, *Preussentum und Sozialismus*, 1919.

[2] Text of John Ball's revolutionary sermon at Blackheath in Wat Tyler's Rebellion, 1387, *Dictionary of Quotations*, Oxford, 1941, p. 527b.

This aspect of relations between the privileged and the under-privileged strata, in the sense of the exploitation of the labour of the under-privileged, is dominant in the consciousness of the revolutionaries and in their militant propaganda. Babeuf, in a letter to Charles Germain, wrote:

'Spéculateurs et marchands, se liguent entre eux pour tenir à leur discrétion le véritable producteur, pour être toujours en position de lui dire: travaille beaucoup, mange peu, ou tu ne mangera pas du tout. Voilà la loi barbare dictée par les capitaux'.[1]

This aspect of human relations also gave rise to the Marxian theory of 'surplus-value'.

'Classes'—explained Lenin—'are groups of people one of which can appropriate the labour of another owing to the different places they occupy in a definite system of social economy.'[2]

For Babeuf, as for the socialists and communists of the nine-teenth and twentieth centuries, the cause of the exploitation of man by man was the concentration of the means of production in the hands of capitalists. But the relationship between the system of ownership and exploitation is not a unilateral one. Wealth or physical force are the sources of exploitation; but when the process of exploitation of the working masses is already under way, it causes added wealth to accrue to the exploiters. The labour of the worker multiplies the wealth or power of those whose wealth or power compel him to labour on for their benefit. This vicious circle was the subject of Shelley's moving exhortations in his 'Song to the Men of England':

> 'Men of England, wherefore plough
> For the lords who lay ye low?
> Wherefore weave with toil and care
> The rich robes your tyrants wear?
> Wherefore feed and clothe and save,
> From the cradle to the grave
> Those ungrateful drones who would

---

[1] Gracchus Babeuf à Charles Germain, 10 Thermidor, an III (1795) – *Pages Choisies de Babeuf*, Paris, Armand Colin, 1935, p. 209.
[2] V. I. Lenin: 'A Great Beginning', in *The Essentials of Lenin*, London, Lawrence & Wishart, 1947, Vol. II, p. 492.

Drain your sweat – nay, drink your blood?

Wherefore, Bees of England, forge
Many a weapon, chain and scourge,
That these stingless drones may spoil
The forced produce of your toil.'

The connexion between wealth and profiteering from other men's labour is a *motif* frequently found in the folk lore of various countries. We are of course familiar with the dichotomic conception of social structure whose supporters – the *avant garde* of the bourgeoisie of the first half of the nineteenth century – attempted to destroy this connexion, while at the same time taking the third relation I have noted as the basis of their dichotomy. This is the postulated division drawn by Saint-Simon between the working class or classes and the idle class, or between the class of producers and the class of consumers who produce nothing. In one passage Saint-Simon, using the same metaphor as his contemporary Shelley, compared the antagonistic classes to bees and drones[1]. But his line of division ran in such a way that the working class also included *les riches travailleurs*: the industrialists, the merchants and the bankers. That is to say, Saint-Simon's class of producer included not only the real 'producers' of Babeuf's dichotomy but also their most severe exploiters. Saint-Simon's 'bees' included the 'drones' and 'drinkers of bees' blood' found in Shelley's manifesto.

Saint-Simon's division between the workers and the non-workers was, in the interests of the victorious class, dissociated from its connexion with the division between the rich and the poor, and even from that between those who rule and those who must obey. Thus it ceased to be an aspect of a vertical order in the social structure. The description of the non-workers as drones was intended to wrench away the last privilege of social prestige. So the very conception of so broadly based a 'working class', in which the economic position of the individual is the measure of his social merit, a conception which fails to consider the stratification within this immense 'class', was to find a corresponding

---

[1] '*Sur la querelle des abeilles et des frélons ou sur la situation respective des producteurs et des consommateurs non-producteurs.*' Cited by Nina Assorodobraj in an interesting study describing this dichotomic aspect of social structure as seen by Saint-Simon and his disciples: 'Elements of class consciousness in the bourgeoisie.' (*Przegląd Socjologiczny*, 1948).

parallel 120 years later in the land of socialism, with the initiation of a campaign against the tendency to equalize individual shares in the national income, at a time when pay-scales were beginning to differ widely within the working population.[1]

## Economic Compulsion and Slavery

If we extend our enquiry into class structure still further back into the past, we find that in ancient times the problem of the relation between those who worked and those who profited by their labour was formulated in both ways, by giving precedence either to the power to command or to economic superiority in the exploitation of others' labour.

According to Aristotle, the basic dichotomy in the social structure was the division between free men and slaves. This was the age-old division which – despite the teaching of the Cynics – was supposed to have a natural basis in the types of human nature. Aristotle was, it is true, more concerned with economic stratification as applied to free citizens, but he regarded the middle state[2] as the best situated, so that his basic distinction between freemen and slaves came out all the more strongly. Moreover, Aristotle was disposed to leave all physical work to the slaves, so that the division in his design for society – that between freeman and slave – would at the same time be the division between non-worker and worker. In the ancient societies of Greece and Rome the class polarity determined by relations of master and slave, that is to say by personal dependence expressed in a relationship of power and a direct and unconditional exploitation, was obviously not coextensive with the division based on the legal position of individuals – that is to say on the division between freeman and slave. The identification of these two divisions (e.g. the treatment of every free citizen as a potential master) made it easier to conceive of the social structure as dichotomic, but it conflicted with reality.

In the Roman Empire, another kind of division began to attract widespread attention after the first century A.D., when the number of slaves was decreasing and their social situation was improving. This was the division of citizens into the 'haves' (the middle and

[1] See p. 112 below.

[2] *Politics*, Book IV, Chapter XI, translated by William Ellis, Everyman's Library, No. 605.

28

upper 'bourgeoisie') and the 'have-nots'. This division was in-stitutionalized in non-economic terms: *honestiores* and *humiliores*[1]; these terms did not however change the actual state of affairs, merely testifying to the prestige of wealth, as do certain passages from the Epistle of St. James.[2]

In the writings of the Fathers of the Church the basic problem of social inequality was not discussed in terms of freeman and slave or of master and slave, but in economic terms. The reflec-tions of St. Augustine on the social structure of the *civitas terrena* do, it is true, refer to both kinds of relationship: master-slave and rich-poor. By use of the dialectic method, this subtle forerunner of Hegel reached conclusions which contradicted his initial assumptions, and justified both the existence of rich and poor and of slavery in the Christian community. But he too regarded social stratification as being based mainly on the relations of ownership. In general, the two strata into which society was divided, accord-ing to the Christian writers of the first five centuries of our era, were those of rich and poor. This was not even a matter of ideo-logy. Such an image of the social structure was common both to those Fathers of the Church who fought in defence of the oppres-sed and had before their eyes a vision of a communistic society, and to those who defended the existing order and the interests of the privileged classes.

For both the former and the latter, the division between workers and non-workers was the result of the division between poor and rich. Whereas Aristotle considered that those social needs which require physical labour could only be met because there were slaves, the Christian writers of the fourth and fifth centuries after Christ saw these needs as being met only 'by virtue of the existence of the poor'. Of the first of his two imagin-ary cities of the rich and of the poor, St. John Chrysostom wrote: 'Now then, in that city of the affluent there will be no manufac-facturer, no builder, no carpenter, no shoe-maker, no baker, no husbandman, no brazier, no rope-maker, nor any other such trade. For who among the rich would ever choose to follow these crafts, seeing that the very men who take them in hand,

---

[1] T. Walek–Czernecki. *Historia gospodarcza świata starożytnego* (Economic History of the Ancient World) Warsaw 1948, Vol. II, pp. 262–3.

[2] Cf. *The Epistle of James*, II, 2–4.

when they become rich, endure no longer the discomfort caused by these works?'[1]

These changes were more than changes of perspective. Over a period of several centuries changes had occurred in social reality which altered the arrangement of human relationships.

St. John Chrysostom even made it quite clear that he was referring to the poor and not to the slaves, since there were no longer any slaves in the Christian community. This was however more a postulate of evolutionary trends than an assertion about the existing state of affairs.[2]

## Correlative Classes

In our examination of the tendency throughout cultural history to conceive the system of human relationships in various complex societies in dichotomic terms, we must make the two following differentiations.

(*a*) In the first place, this dichotomic presentation may serve to underline the antagonistic relations existing in the society, relations where one side is 'on top', the other 'at the bottom', where one exploits the other, where one rules and the other obeys, without however assuming that those who are above and those who are below are two vast classes, opposed to each other as wholes. There may be a number of classes in such a society, but the point is simply that each of them is correlated in a similar manner to some other class; for instance, the social position of the serf is determined by his relationship to the landowner, just as the position of the apprentice is determined by his relationship to the master craftsman in the guild.

(*b*) The second possibility is that the whole society may be visualized as a collectivity with a structure containing two strata. In the examples hitherto considered, we have been concerned with this latter possibility, and have looked for images of society conceived in terms of a dichotomic scheme.

Both these ways of conceiving of class divisions can be found in the Communist Manifesto. The first appears in the image of past

[1] 'On the First Letter to the Corinthians, Homily XXXIV' (translated by members of the English Church) in *A Library of Fathers of the Holy Catholic Church, anterior to the Division of the East and West*, Vol. V, Oxford, 1840.

[2] *Op. cit.*, 'On the Acts of the Apostles, Homily XI', cited by G. Walter, *Les Origines du Communisme*, Paris, 1931, pp. 159 and 162.

societies; the second in the conception of the evolutionary tendency of the society of that time:

'The history of all hitherto-existing society is the history of class struggles. Freeman and slave, patrician and plebeian, lord and serf, guild master and journeyman, in a word, oppressor and oppressed, stood in constant opposition to one another, carried on an uninterrupted, now hidden, now open fight. . . .

In the earlier epochs of history, we find almost everywhere a complicated arrangement of society into various orders, a manifold gradation of social rank. . . .

Our epoch, the epoch of the bourgeoisie, possesses, however, this distinctive feature: it has simplified the class antagonism. Society as a whole is more and more splitting up into two great hostile camps, into two great classes directly facing each other: Bourgeoisie and Proletariat.'[1]

The dichotomic conception of social structure is a generalisation for the entire society of a two-term asymmetric relation in which one side is privileged at the expense of the other. In this conception society is divided into two correlative and diametrically opposed classes in such a way that each of these classes is characterized by the relation of its members to the members of the opposed class.

It has been said earlier that this asymmetric relation can assume three forms: first the relation of power, second the relation involving the exploitation of the labour of others and third the relation denoted by the expression 'rich and poor' or 'haves and have-nots'. One might think that this third aspect of the dichotomy does not give any grounds for speaking of correlative classes. For the rulers cannot be defined without reference to their relation with those who are ruled, but the rich can be described without reference to their relation to the poor. In this case we should be concerned not with correlative classes, but with a polarized form of a gradation of property, similar to the three-term scheme which will be discussed in the next chapter.

It seems to me, however, that this would be an incorrect interpretation of the dichotomic scheme in the social consciousness. The dichotomic conception of the relation of property is in fact an

---

[1] 'Manifesto of the Communist Party', ME, Vol. I, pp. 33–34.

expression of the belief that we are here concerned with real, correlative and opposed relations and not only with different ways of formulating them; and that the existence of the rich is conditioned by the existence of the poor and conversely. This dependence can be explained on the one hand by the limited amount of wealth (if one man owns too much, another must go without) and, on the other hand, by those aspects of the dichotomy which concern the relationships of exploitation and power, and which are causally connected with the relation between rich and poor. Nearly fifteen hundred years before Proudhon, St John Chrysostom declared that the root and origin of private riches was always to be found in some injustice or rapine.[1]

## Conditions that Favour Dichotomic Conceptions

In the societies which we are considering, societies that are differentiated at least to the degree of the Greek *polis*, the sharp dichotomic division between those on top and those at the bottom is usually found to conflict with everyday experience, if this division is in absolute terms as the only one of real significance for the social situation of individuals.

When we are concerned with a division based on the relations of ownership (rich and poor), the dichotomy usually clashes with the fact that there are gradations of wealth with a whole range of intermediate positions. When estate or caste privileges are taken as the principle of division, the clash with reality is apparent everywhere where the estate or caste hierarchy is not confined to the division between freemen and slaves or between nobles and the ordinary people. After all, even in the democratic Greek republics there were metics as well as citizens.

Often two dichotomies based on different principles of division will interlock or clash. In certain situations one or the other dichotomy will seem the more important. The overlapping of two mutually incompatible dichotomic divisions leads to the establishment of at least a third category, and thus a three-term scheme emerges. If we put the two different versions of the Vedic myth of the origin of castes together, the Vaishyas emerge as a group separated from the two higher castes by Brahma's navel and distinguished from the Shudra by a line drawn at Brahma's knees. In the image of Greek society, we arrive at a three-class system

[1] *Ibid.* I Timothy, Homily XII, cited by Walter, *op. cit.,* p. 150.

through the overlapping of the dichotomic division into freemen and slaves with the dichotomic division drawn between those who work and those who do not.[1]

Similarly, a combination of two dichotomic divisions complicates the image of modern society. If we compare Babeuf's dichotomic conception of social structure with that of Saint-Simon, it will be seen that Babeuf allocates to the class of exploiters a group which Saint-Simon sees as opposed to the idle class, and which he classifies as a part of the class of *producteurs*, along with all those whom Babeuf defines as the exploited class of real producers. In the Marxian conception of social classes, conceived as groups determined by their relation to the means of production, we are concerned with three criteria of a dichotomic division. Two of these criteria are regarded as particularly important; first, the ownership or non-ownership of the means of production; and second the employment or non-employment of a hired labour force. And here again the overlapping of these two divisions, each of them important, leads to a three-term system through the separation of the class of those who own the means of production but do not employ hired labour.

Nor is this merely a matter of theoretical classification. During long-drawn-out social struggles the front line shifts according to the shifting loyalties of various groups, which ally themselves with those at the bottom against those on top, or *vice versa*, according to the course of events. Various coalitions of classes arise in turn, and there may even be temporary alliances between the upper and the lower classes against the middle class. Such phenomena force one to conclude that many kinds of class divisions co-exist, and they complicate the image of social structure. Instances of this may be sought equally well in the history of the late mediaeval Italian republics, the Hussite wars, the Cromwellian or French Revolutions, the social struggles in the France of the mid-nineteenth century or the early Roman Republic from the time of Appius Claudius at the end of the third century B.C.

Despite all these clashes with reality, however, the dichotomic conception of social structure is so widespread in the history of class societies that it seems worth while devoting some thought to the sort of conditions that favour the creation of such an image;

[1] Cf. Aristotle, *op. cit.*, p. 88.

the more so because this propensity to conceive of the social structure in dichotomic terms is not peculiar to any one class.

Leaving aside a certain psychological factor – the universal tendency to concentrate on extremes – we may distinguish two categories of circumstances that favour such dichotomic conceptions.

The first category consists of those characteristics of a social structure that cause certain societies to be objectively closer to a dichotomic scheme than others. For instance, in a slave system there will be a great distance between the social position of the slave and that of even the lowest groups in the free population. Such relations are to be found in the first half of the nineteenth century in the Southern States of North America, and they compare unfavourably with the situation of the slaves in many countries of the ancient world at various periods. In modern societies, a situation of this kind may be found in conjunction with a high degree of economic polarisation, with a blatant coexistence of wealth and poverty.

The second category consists of the sort of circumstances that aid the image of a dichotomic social structure to appeal to certain social classes or to promote their interests. I will try to indicate some circumstances of this kind.

(1). In societies which are characterized by grievous oppression or exploitation of one class by another, the antagonistic relation tends to conceal the existence of other groups and other conflicts from the oppressed class. This particular antagonistic relation seems to the oppressed to apply generally throughout the society. Such situations are encountered in various social systems. For the serf, society is composed above all of lords and serfs; for the industrial worker, it is composed of workers and capitalists. As for other groups, their existence is known, but the knowledge of their existence is shifted on to the margin of awareness when there is a desire to emphasize those aspects of the social structure which are most important from a class perspective. In any case, the differentiation of a hierarchy of privileged classes is meaningless even in normal circumstances from the viewpoint of the lowest class. The young Engels wrote:

'In speaking of the bourgeoisie I include the so-called aristocracy, for this is a privileged class, an aristocracy, only in contrast with the bourgeoisie, not in contrast with the proletariat. The proletarian sees in both only the property-holder, i.e., the bourgeois. Before the privilege of property all other privileges vanish.'[1]

(2). As far as the privileged classes are concerned, if the domination of a particular class is firmly established, and the barriers separating it from other strata are rigid and almost impenetrable, as in an estate system, the sharp contrast drawn by the members of the dominating class between themselves and the rest of society can be an expression of their effort to increase the distance between their class and all the others. For the situation of the dominating class appears so secure that there is no need for it to seek allies in the strata below by means of a 'divide and rule' policy. In these conditions, the increase of social distance leads to an extension of the privileges enjoyed by the dominating class. Such a trend was clearly revealed amongst the representatives of the Polish nobility (*szlachta*) after its victories of the sixteenth century. At this period in the Polish Republic a class dictatorship was realized in a more literal sense than the class dictatorship found in the countries where the proletariat has been victorious in our century. In his treatise *The Police*, Orzechowski[2] transposed the ancient division of the population into freemen and slaves in such a manner that only the Polish *szlachta* was seen as corresponding to the free citizens of the ancient city-states, and the basic division between the *szlachta* and the rest became the division between those who give orders and those whose lot it is only to obey.[3]

The dichotomic structure is seen as a programme of democracy confined to the nobility. This democracy may be victorious, as in Poland, or only postulated. In a work published posthumously outside France after the death of Louis XIV,[4] Henri de Boulainvilliers outlined a theory of the racial division between the French nobility and the remainder of the population of that country. Here the sharpness of the division was connected with the defence of the liberties of the nobility, which were being strangled by the

[1] F. Engels, 'The Conditions of the Working-Class in England', published in K. Marx and F. Engels, *On Britain*, Moscow, Foreign Languages Publishing House, 1953, pp. 310–311.

[2] Stanislaw Orzechowski was a political writer of the sixteenth century.

[3] Cf. M. Ossowska; *Moralność mieszczańska* ('Bourgeois Mentality') Łódź 1956, p. 38f.

[4] *Histoire de l'ancien gouvernement de France*, The Hague, 1727.

absolutism of the French Kings, who, according to the author, looked for support to the Gallo-Roman plebeians in order to carry out their plans.

In liberated America, a dichotomic conception of the social structure was put forward by Alexander Hamilton, the political opponent of Jefferson. His desire was to transform the American plutocracy into a closed class modelled on the European aristocracy. Hamilton used a conception of a bistratal structure as an argument to support an aristocratic senate composed of representatives of the plutocracy elected for a life term.

'All communities divide themselves into the few and the many. The first are rich and well-born and the other the mass of the people who seldom judge or determine right.'[1]

But the voice of Hamilton was the voice of a man engrossed in contemplation of the past. It found no echo in the new republic. The American Creed, on which American children are reared, that creed which is so advantageous for the ruling system, sprang from other premises. As in other capitalistic countries, here too the propaganda disseminated by the ruling class is opposed to sharp divisions in the mode of perception of the social structure because it is opposed to the idea of the class struggle. In the United States one must look elsewhere for the dichotomic aspect of the social structure. One must look to the relation between the Negro and the white population. In this sphere the dichotomy has endured until the present time; as we know, there is no intermediate category between Negroes and whites in the caste-like structure of the Southern States.[2]

During periods of class struggle, the tendency to conceive the existing system in terms of a dichotomic scheme and to overlook intermediate positions between the contending groups becomes an important propaganda factor for those whose strategy is best suited by the stressing of a single front line. In 1789 it was desirable to cement together all the classes within the French third estate for the fight against the aristocracy and the *ancien régime*. In his famous treatise *'Qu'est-ce que le tiers état?'*, the Abbé Sieyès took up the conception of racial opposition between the German

[1] Beard, C. & M., *The Rise of American Civilization*, Vol. I, New York, 1930, p.316.

[2] See pp. 108–110 below.

aristocracy and the Gallo-Romans who constituted the remainder of the population. This division had been outlined by Henri de Boulainvilliers for entirely different motives in the days of Louis XIV. In 1795, Babeuf divided the population of France into 24 million real producers, deprived of the means of satisfying their basic needs adequately, and one million exploiters; he did not perceive those who were in an intermediate economic position. Marx and Engels, whose strategy of the class struggle also imposed a dichotomic image of society, projected this image into the future without distorting contemporary reality, and postulated the polarization of society as the outcome of further historical development.[1] The dichotomic Marxian way of perceiving the social structure was later to be enriched by a dichotomic perception of culture not unconnected with the militant functions of the Marxian doctrine. This was to find expression, *inter alia,* in Lenin's theory of the 'two trends in culture'.

In this case the simplified perception of class structure was not only a matter of 'social perspective' as in the earlier examples; it was simultaneously the result of the consciously militant strategy of a militant movement.

---

[1] Engels visualized such a polarization through the disappearance of the lower middle-class (*Ruin der kleinen Mittelklasse*) nearly three years before the appearance of the 'Communist Manifesto' (*op. cit.* p. 319).

# Chapter III

## THE SCHEME OF GRADATION[1]

*Intermediate Classes in a Two-Fold Interpretation.*

IN THE last part of the last chapter I spoke of the circumstances which complicate the image of the social structure and impose the conception of intermediate classes; this conception clashes with the tendency to conceive of social reality in terms of a dichotomic scheme. As we know, facts are powerless against stereotypes supported by emotional motivations. An intellectual scheme that is rooted in the social consciousness may within certain limits successfully withstand the test of reality. In time of need, arguments or interpretations can always be found to invalidate inconvenient facts. For instance, it is possible to blot out the variety of class antagonisms in the image of the social structure by interpreting only one of these antagonisms as essential and the remainder as 'quarrels within the family'.

There are however a variety of social causes which give added significance to these facts and which make them sufficiently impressive to ensure that social reality should appear in a form more complicated than that which is imposed by a dichotomic scheme. As we have seen, it is in the interest of certain classes to stress the sharp division of society into two opposing parts, but this may

[1] The term 'gradation' (Polish *gradacja*) is retained in the translation, instead of using the more familiar 'ranking', because the author clearly differentiates between them. 'Rank', as used in American and English sociology, refers to the relative position or status of members of a group with respect to each other as assigned and evaluated by themselves or by the researcher. Therefore, a sequence of degrees in rank is either something subjectively perceived or intuitively assessed. But not every sequence of degrees in rank is based on a subjective evaluation. When individuals are ranked according to their education or wealth, an objectively valid criterion of rank is applied. 'Gradation' denotes both the subjectively evaluated and the objectively measured rank and differentiates them by qualifying the latter as 'simple' and the former as 'synthetic gradation' (note by Dr. Z. Jordan).

clash with the interests of other classes. The different ways of perceiving class structure cannot however always be explained in this way. One can without difficulty find examples of societies in which, within the same class milieu, dichotomic and trichotomous perceptions of the same society are interchangeable, according to the situation. For instance, St. John Chrysostom, whose immense literary heritage gives so realistic a picture of the social life of his time, divided Christian society into three classes[1] in the early part of his ministry; several years later, however, after his appointment as Bishop of Constantinople, he simplified the social structure in his parable about the city of the rich and the city of the poor, distinguishing only the rich and the poor, without an intermediate class. The intersection of a dichotomic scheme and schemes of multiple division found in the works of Marx will be considered in a subsequent chapter.

The introduction of intermediate classes does not preclude the possibility of interpreting social structure in very diverse ways, because the intermediate classes can play differing roles in the image of the society. There are two extreme conceptions of the intermediate classes, to which there correspond two perceptions of a trichotomous structure: one of these is associated with Marx, the other with Aristotle.

According to the first conception, the diametrically opposed classes are the basic classes in the social structure. The middle class is less important and less enduring. It is a typically marginal class and if sharp conflicts arise it joins with one or other of the two opposite classes. Its existence does not deprive the social structure of its dichotomic character, but merely blunts its sharpness. One might say that in terms of this conception the trichotomous scheme arising out of the existence of a middle class is a deviation from the ideal type of the dichotomic division.

According to the second conception, the middle class constitutes the basic class while the rich and poor classes are deviations from the mean position in the scale. In Aristotle's trichotomous scheme, it is not the middle class but the extreme classes that are in some sense marginal.

Between these mutually exclusive interpretations of a trichotomous structure, and between the Marxian and Aristotelian conceptions of the middle class, there is room for a 'neutral' inter-

[1] *Ibid. On St. Matthew, Homily LXXXV.*

pretation in which all three parts of society would be regarded as being of more or less equal order.

In discussing the Aristotelian conception, we must of course remember that Aristotle did not intend this to be a description of contemporary reality; in his *Politics* he gave differing presentations of the social structures of particular Greek city-states. The dominance of the middle class in the social structure was for him, however, a prerequisite of the good society.

'In every city the people are divided into three sorts; the very rich, the very poor, and those who are between them. If this is universally admitted, that the mean is best, it is evident that even in point of fortune mediocrity is to be preferred .... It is plain, then, that the most perfect political community must be amongst those who are in the middle rank, and those states are best instituted wherein these are a larger and more respectable part, if possible, than both the others, or, if that cannot be, at least than either of them separately.'[1]

When St. John Chrysostom described the Christian society of Antioch at the end of the fourth century A.D. in terms of a trichotomous scheme, he attributed to the middle class a position both of numerical predominance and of the greatest importance from the viewpoint of social benefits. In his view, the middle class, which lived modestly but did not go hungry, made up the great majority of the population. It consisted of those who work. The rich did not work; while the class of the poor in this earlier version appear to consist in part of the unemployed or under-employed proletariat and in part of the professional beggars, whose numbers were very high in the cities of that time.

In a somewhat later book, an anonymous Pelagian treatise *On Wealth*, which, is according to Walter[2], *inter alia* a polemical reply to St. Augustine's argument in defence of the owners of wealth, society is again divided into three classes. As with St. John Chrysostom, the criterion of the division was the degree of wealth. In its formulation this trichotomous gradation recalls Aristotle's triads. Also reminiscent of Aristotle's philosophy is the proposition that wealth (the situation of owning more than one needs) and poverty (when one owns less than one needs) are states which are not in accordance with nature, whereas only

[1] Aristotle, *Politics*, Book IV, Chapter XI, translated by William Ellis, Everyman's Library, No. 605, pp. 126–7.
[2] *Les origines du Communisme*, G. Walter, Paris, 1931, p. 242.

the mean between these extremes is such a state. This is the state in which one owns as much as one needs and no more. The numerical proportions in this trichotomous system are, however, different from those found in Chrysostom's homily from Antioch.

In Chrysostom's version, the middle class was as large as it would, according to the results of several surveys, appear to be in the United States today.[1] On the other hand, the author of the anonymous treatise 'On Wealth' gave proportions that are nearer to the Marxian analyses. He saw the greater part of the society as composed of those who lived in need and poverty, while he saw the cause of their poverty in the existence of a small number of rich people.

At the beginning of modern capitalism in the Italian cities during the Renaissance, the conception of a trichotomous gradation was also to find a theoretical foundation in the philosophy of Aristotle. Later this conception achieved a wide circulation in the capitalistic societies of the 19th century, but without going back to Aristotle.

## The Scheme of Gradation of Social Classes

If we conceive of the social structure in a dichotomic scheme, we see society as split into two opposing classes, between which an asymmetrical relation of dependence holds. Each of these classes is characterized by its relationship to the other. The conception of intermediate classes suggests a different sort of scheme. This second way of conceiving social structure I shall call the scheme of gradation: it is a scheme of multiple divisions but, as we shall see later, it is not the only kind of multi-divisional scheme. In this scheme society is perceived in the form of a stratified system of three or more classes, of which each is higher or lower than the others in the same respect. Here too each class is defined in terms of its relations to other classes, but the relation is conceived not as a relation of dependence but merely as an ordering relation.

## Simple Gradation

Here we must distinguish between two schemes of gradation: simple gradation and synthetic gradation. By simple gradation in

---

[1] See p. 103 below.

the system of social classes, I understand a conception of social structure in which the relation of higher and lower classes is based on the grading of some objectively measurable characteristic. Concretely, we are concerned here with the gradation of wealth, the amount of property or the size of a person's share in the national income. In this conception, it is their relative wealth which determines people's class membership, and it is relative wealth that assigns to the different classes their respective positions in the vertical order.

The concept of simple gradation applies only to those instances in which one criterion alone is decisive. Where two or more incommensurable criteria are involved in fixing the levels in the social structure, the situation undergoes an essential change in certain respects which we shall be discussing shortly. For this reason, I thought it necessary to introduce the concept of synthetic gradation.

In the scheme of simple gradation, the economic criterion is naturally not the only one that can be applied. One might for instance set up a gradation of classes with educational levels as the basis of the gradation. Such conceptions have, however, played no role in the history of social thought or at least not in the sphere of European culture. We have encountered no such conceptions of social structure in the social consciousness. The level of education is at times an important dimension in a synthetic gradation, but outside some social milieux in ancient China it does not play any part in a class gradation based on one criterion only. When therefore we speak of a simple gradation in conceptions of social structure we are referring only to a scheme of economic gradation.

The scheme of simple gradation which we encountered in Aristotle's *Politics*, in the *Homilies* of St. John Chrysostom, and in the Pelagian treatise *On Wealth* has sometimes been embodied in political institutions. In ancient times, a timocratic system, that is to say an estate structure based on the principles of economic gradation, namely on the census of property, was sometimes established on the ruins of the former estate system, which was based on lineage and tribal ties. A timocracy was an estate structure in which status was not pre-determined by birth. The classic example of it is to be found in the reforms of Solon, in which the citizens of Athens were divided into four classes according to the size of their income, each class having institutionally-established political privileges and obligations.

Other Greek republics experienced similar reforms, in which the criterion of simple gradation became the basis of an institutionalized division of the citizen body into social classes. The same was true of Rome.[1] Again at the beginning of this century, a sociological writer maintained that in democratic Switzerland people marry and maintain social relations within the boundaries of their income-tax categories. If this ironic observation be correct we should have here a timocratic social structure operating as a normative factor in the life of the collectivity. In conditions of relative stability, classes which are differentiated on the basis of an economic criterion have sometimes been known to achieve institutionalized status through customs modelled on estate distinctions. In pre-Revolutionary America, members of the small class of rich planters and merchants were, as persons of quality, exempt from corporal punishment, and men who belonged to this group were entitled to use the title 'Mr.', 'Gentleman' or 'Gent'; these titles were scrupulously emphasized on their grave-stones. In New England, persons of moderate wealth, owning their own means of production, called one another 'Goodman' and 'Goodwife', while hired men and propertyless persons were addressed by their given names.[2]

Where the degree of wealth is a basic criterion individuals of the same occupational group may be assigned different social roles. In his *Le parfait negociant*, published in 1675, Savary drew a sharp distinction between the wholesaler and the retailer.[3] Two centuries earlier, Villon, when he was a fugitive from the law,

[1] The most important reference here is the reform of Servius Tullius. In the first centuries of the Roman Republic, the citizens were divided into six classes on the basis of the property census; according to Livy, the franchise law gave the first class (citizens whose property exceeded 100,000 ases in value) a definitive majority of votes, while the citizens of the lowest property class were exempt from military service and were called *proletarii*, a name inherited by the working class of our time. Later, when the Roman Republic was transformed into a principate, Augustus was guided by the same principle; in his reforms he made membership of the senatorial order dependent on a property census assessment of one million sestertii; the qualification for membership of the equestrian order, which Walek-Czernecki regards as the equivalent of the English upper-middle class, was set at 400,000 sestertii (cf. Walek-Czernecki, *op. cit.*, Vol. II, pp. 253–4.

[2] Cf. C. Mayer: 'Recent Changes in the Class Structure of the United States', *Transactions of the Third World Congress of Sociology*, Vol. III, London 1956, p. 68.

[3] Cf. M. Ossowska: *Moralność mieszczańska* (Bourgeois Morality) pp. 145–6.

wrote a verse on the old anecdote about Alexander of Macedon
and the pirate:

> 'The Emperor addressed him: "Why
> Art thou a robber on the main?"
> To this the pirate made reply:
> "Why dost thou so my trade disdain?
> Because 'tis known I scour the brine
> In a small narrow ship of war?
> Had I an armament like thine,
> I'd be like thee, an emperor." '[1]

The scheme of simple gradation divided the peasant community
in many European countries into the categories of yeomen,
cottagers and village paupers, or into kulaks, middle peasants and
poor peasants.[2] In the latter case, the gradation of property was
mainly a gradation of landownership measured in morgen and
hectares.

## Synthetic Gradation.

When the social stratification of the capitalistic countries of
Europe and America is discussed in terms of a class-hierarchy in
non-Marxist circles, a simple gradation of classes determined by
economic criteria is sometimes meant. For instance, the British
economist, Professor Lionel Robbins, introduced the concept of
inferior income groups instead of the concept of the proletariat
in his study of class relationships.[3] In France, a questionnaire
issued by the Institute of Public Opinion in 1947 presented the
social structure of France in terms of a scheme of economic
gradation.[4] But when in England, France or America one speaks
of the middle, upper-middle and upper classes, or when the

[1] Francois Villon, 'The Testament', XVIII, *Poems*; trans. Norman Cameron,
Jonathan Cape, 1952.

[2] Until the last war in some provinces of Poland a peasant in this last category was
called *komornik*: this meant that he had no cottage of his own but rented a small
room (*komora*) from a *kmieć* (yeoman) or a *zagrodnik* (cottager). The Russian terms
*kulak, sredniak* and *bedniak* (*bedny*, – poor) have become widely known outside
Russia thanks to Lenin's writings.

[3] *The Economic Basis of Class Conflict*, Macmillan, 1939, p. 26 and elsewhere.

[4] The question ran: 'Estimez-vous que vous appartenez à la classe riche, à la
classe pauvre, à la class moyenne, plutôt riche, ou à la classe moyenne, plutôt pauvre?'
(Quoted by R. Centers: *The Psychology of Social Class*, Princeton University Press
1949, p. 223.)

number of social classes in the United States is debated in American periodicals, the class-hierarchy involved is not constructed according to a simple economic gradation.

Thus some American social scientists distinguish between 'social class' and 'economic class',[1] while Centers, the author of that important and interesting study *The Psychology of Social Class*, introduces a distinction between social stratum and social class. For Centers, social stratification is based on some objective criterion which is arbitrarily adopted as the basis of ranking. Such a stratification will therefore fit into our scheme of simple gradation, although theoretically for Centers the ordering relation need not be the relation of wealth.[2] On the other hand, this writer conceives of classes as groups in which membership is determined not by a single objective criterion but by class consciousness, which may comprise many kinds of criteria. The same applies to the hierarchical system of social classes, which in contradistinction to Centers's concept of stratification is not based on the gradation of a single measurable characteristic.

The perception of a stratified social structure divided into 'lower, middle and upper classes', which are not understood as a simple gradation, would appear to be brought into use at times when new hierarchies are taking shape after an estate system is overcome, and when the concept of 'high society' ceases to be identified with the closed circle of the hereditary aristocracy. Outside the sphere of Marxian influence, and above all in the Anglo-Saxon countries and in Latin America, this grading terminology survives to the present day both in everyday language and in the press and theoretical studies.

In Victorian and twentieth-century England, the classification of individuals according to a tetratomic class system (upper, upper-middle, lower-middle, lower) was universally accepted in bourgeois and petit-bourgeois milieux at least until the second World War. In East Germany, the traces of a division into an upper, middle and lower class have even outlasted the change in the social system, if we are to judge by a communiqué issued by

[1] Cf. H. Cantril: 'Identification with Social and Economic Class', *Journal of Abnormal and Social Psychology*, 1943.

[2] 'Since stratification is merely a descriptive term for the existence of high and low in a society, it is theoretically possible to have as many kinds of stratification as one can discover objective criteria for defining' (*op. cit.*, p. 15).

the Council of Ministers of the German Democratic Republic on
11 June 1953. This speaks of the 'middle estate', whose composition does not coincide with that of the Marxian petit bourgeoisie
in the sense of being a class determined by a certain relation to the
means of production.

In the United States we are continually coming across such a
scheme of gradation in field research and theoretical discussion
about that country's social structure. The number of classes
defined in terms of a ranking scale varies from three (upper,
middle and lower)[1] to six (upper-upper, lower-upper, upper-
middle, lower-middle, upper-lower, lower-lower).[2]

In surveys concerned with class membership, the scheme is
often complicated by the introduction of a term which does not
directly denote a rank in the gradation. This is the term 'working
class'. The term 'lower class' has been found to carry a pejorative
implication. People do not care to admit to membership of such a
class, and thus an immense percentage represent themselves as
members of the middle class. For this reason, the trichotomous
division may be enlarged by inserting the category 'working class'
between 'middle class' and 'lower class'.[3] This category may be
interpreted in different ways; it may be seen as a rank in the
stratification, some sort of lower-middle or upper-lower class,
or as a group specially distinguished by the nature of its occupation and the source of its income. In the first interpretation
we are concerned with a scheme of gradation, while the second
involves a scheme of heterogeneous construction or rather
the intersection of two different schemes. A similar tetratomic scheme was used in West Germany in 1946, but here the
term 'workers' class' (*Arbeitklasse*) took the place of 'working
class'.[4]

In a study of social structure carried out in Sweden in 1943, the
questionnaire distinguished four social classes: upper, upper-
middle, middle and the class of 'workers and all those who occupy
a similar social position.' In this case the ranking connotation of

---

[1] See Centers, *op. cit.*, pp. 30–31, and Hollingshead, 'Trends in Social Stratification', *American Sociological Review*, 1952, Vol. 17, pp. 679–686.
[2] This is the scheme of W. L. Warner and P. S. Lunt (*The Social Life of a Modern
Community*, Yale University Press, 1941); it is also applied *inter alios* by the authors of
*Deep South*, University of Chicago Press, 1941.
[3] Cf. Centers, *op. cit.*, p. 32 and pp. 211–213.
[4] *Ibid.*, p. 255.

this fourth class is quite clear. It occupies the place of the lower class which was not listed.

The distinction between economic class and social class in the framework of a scheme of gradation is based on the assumption that social status is determined by several factors, and that, within certain limits at least, these factors may compensate for one another. Lack of education or inferior birth can be offset by economic power: a *nouveau riche* must be richer than other people in the class to which he aspires. Inadequate income may to a certain degree be offset by high social status, or by the fact of having wealthy forebears. As Halbwachs wrote: *La qualité de riche ne se perd pas avec la richesse.*[1]

The power of the dollar enters into the European stereotype of the American as the ultimate measuring-stick of all values.

'In America money makes the man; in England, at least until recently, one had to wait – money made only one's children' – wrote Roy Lewis and Alan Maude in *The English Middle Classes.*[2] This contention is of course false if one take it literally, and not merely as being an expression of a 'comparable trait'. One must have the appropriate income in order to be a member of the English upper class, just as in the case of the American upper class. But in neither country is the size of a person's income a sufficient qualification for membership of the upper class, unless that income vastly exceeds the level acceptable as a necessary condition for membership.

In their *Yankee City Series* Warner and Lunt found a high correlation between class status and type of occupation.

'Class and occupation are closely interrelated, but it is a mistake to classify all professional people at the top of the heap and all workers at the bottom; far too many factors contribute to a person's social status for such arbitrary ranking to be exact and accurate.'[3]

Wherever the number of variables had to be limited for technical reasons, indeed, these writers introduced the following indices of class membership: occupation, source of income, rental value of housing and residential area.[4] In his investigation in Detroit

---

[1] M. Halbwachs: *Les cadres sociaux de mémoire*, Paris, Alcan, 1935, p. 340.

[2] Phoenix House, London, 1949, p. 19.

[3] *The Social Life of a Modern Community*, p. 262.

[4] W. L. Warner: 'A Methodology for the Study of Social Class', in the joint compilation *Social Structure* (ed. Meyer Fortes), Oxford, 1949.

G. H. Lenski considered two factors on which social status depends and which can be quantified, namely income and education, and two factors for which the scale of social prestige has no objective indicators, namely occupation and ethnic origin. In the latter case he was concerned with such ethnic groups as Americans of Anglo-Saxon origin, Scandinavians, Irish, Germans, Italians, Poles, Jews, Mexicans and Negroes: groups whose variety and prestige hierarchy are characteristic for the great industrial cities of the United States.[1] L. Reissman determined class membership by means of three variables: occupation, income and education.[2]

In Warner and Lunt's work, two of the indices used in assessing class status, those of the type of residence and residential area, are connected with the style of life. 'Conspicuous consumption', which was discussed by Veblen in his classic work,[3] is also concerned with the style of life as a criterion of class affiliation.

We know how important was the style of life in the class hierarchies of European bourgeois societies. This is shown for instance in Goblot's *La barrière et le niveau* (1925) and the Polish *romans des moeurs* of the late nineteenth and early twentieth centuries. Even details are significant in this respect. 'We middle-class people' – the proprietress of a modest boarding house in London told me in 1934 – 'read the *Daily Mail* or the *Daily Express*. Upper middle-class people read *The Times*'.[4] This statement was not a matter of political affiliation, since all three papers were more or less conservative in tone.

In Latin America social class and economic class are very far from being identical. R. C. Beals writes:

'Sources of wealth, family position, class consciousness, the status significance of various occupations and the deeply entrenched dichotomy between those who work with their hands and those who do not, all these retain a great symbolical value.'[5]

[1] 'Status Crystallisation', *American Sociological Review*, 1954.
[2] 'For the purposes of this analysis, class is determined by means of three commonly used variables – occupation, income and education'. 'Class, Leisure and Social Participation', *A.S.R.* 1954, p. 79.
[3] *The Theory of the Leisure Class*, New York, 1899.
[4] This association between class affiliation and readership has more recently been emphasized in the advertising slogan *Top People Read the Times*.
[5] 'Social Stratification in Latin America', *A.J.S.* 1953, Vol. LVII, p. 330.

There are some societies in which a gradation which appears to be based on one criterion only is in fact a synthetic gradation. This may occur if the social stratification is established on the basis of the occupations of individuals, beginning with unskilled workers and ending with members of the professions or big business. Hollingshead, for instance, has used such a gradation of 'socio-economic groups'.[1] But the occupational hierarchy does not coincide with the income hierarchy and therefore the gradation must be based on a synthesis of the various factors which is carried out in the social consciousness.[2] Such a synthesis depends on the milieu in which it is made. Thus the occupational hierarchy accepted by Hollingshead is not identical with that employed by Centers.

## Property Privileges in a Synthetic Gradation

Style of life is not an attribute which is subject to ranking according to some uniform scale, like wealth or education. As a class characteristic, however, style of life consists above all in the standards and forms of consumption. The style of life is reflected in the individual budget. The size of the budget does not of course presuppose a certain style of life, for the same money can be spent in very different ways once the so-called minimum of subsistence is exceeded. On the other hand, certain styles of life do presuppose a corresponding income-level. Thus it would appear that the scale of expenditure can serve as an indicator of the style of life. In this connection, people often speak of the way of life on an 'appropriate level'. If upper-middle class people aspire to model themselves on the upper class, they must have adequate resources to realize these aspirations, beginning with the purchase or lease of a house in a suitable and expensive district. A gentleman is not supposed to care about money. But one must have money in order to be able not to care about it. One must also have money in order to be lavish. In the *Gazeta Krakowska* (Cracow Gazette) of 9 January 1811, there appeared an advertisement concerning the visit of the travelling exhibition of wax

---

[1] 'Trends in Social Stratification', *A.S.R.* 1952, p. 682 and elsewhere.
[2] L. Corey mentions several such factors in his study 'The Middle Class', *The Antioch Review*, 1945 (republished in 'Class Status and Power', ed. R. Bendix and S. M. Lipset, 'The Free Press', Routledge and Glencoe, 1953, pp. 378-380).

models made by the Milanese craftsman Pecchi; this included the following list of entrance fees: 'Persons of the first estate will pay according to their pleasure. Distinguished personages will pay 2 zlotys; children and servants 1 zloty'.[1]

In the establishment of a synthetic gradation one must take into account both the income-level and the amount of expenditure needed to maintain a certain style of life. Thus the privileges of wealth condition class status in two ways: first, with regard to the 'timocratic' function of money (the relative amount of wealth being a direct factor of social prestige); second in that an appropriate income is a necessary condition for maintaining a style of life on an appropriate level. The latter consideration has frequently been advanced to defend the viewpoint that people from the upper strata should have higher incomes.

The relationship holds both ways. The style of life is also taken into account in the gradation as evidence of wealth, and thus with regard to the 'timocratic' function of money which has just been mentioned. The same is true of education, particularly of the costly type; for instance, education abroad in countries with a disadvantageous exchange rate, or in England expensive education in such establishments as Eton and Harrow or Oxford and Cambridge used to be (and in many cases still is) valued not only for the personal qualifications which accrued to the student, but also, unless he held a scholarship or bursary, as an indication of the high financial status of his parents.

Money can fulfil yet a third function in a social hierarchy. The income level may be regarded as an outward indication of the individual's social role. An instance of this is found in the Soviet Union, where it is accepted that each receives his share in the national income according to his merits. According to this assumption social merit, and thus an individual's position in the scale of social roles, can be measured by the income received by each citizen. This view point was not alien to capitalist thought. The followers of Saint-Simon appealed to social merit to justify the high incomes of industrialists. Wealth was the measure of divine grace; and thus also the measure of perseverance in the service of God amongst the English Puritans and in the Puritan sects in America. And several centuries before the Puritans, the wealthy Italian merchant, Giovanni Morelli, (1371–1441) de-

[1] K. Bakowski, *Kronika Krakowska* (Cracow Chronicle), 1796–1842.

clared that God apportions out worldly goods in proportion to an individual's merits.[1]

If the perception of the social structure in an estate society included a scheme of gradation in addition to the estate hierarchy, this was a simple economic gradation. Following Aristotle's example, people were divided up not only into the categories of citizens, metics and slaves, or nobility, burgesses and peasants, but also into rich, poor and those of moderate means. A synthetic gradation would, on the other hand, appear to be an indirect effect of the official abolition of estate privileges. Estate privileges and relationships gave way to a system based in principle on purely economic relationships; but certain estate traditions did not lose their vitality or were revived when the new system attained stability.[2] Descent as a determinant of social status is a relic of an estate or caste system. But descent from a wealthy family has continued to play a part in determining social status in bourgeois democracies. Style of life, which is one of the criteria in modern class hierarchies, is in certain respects a legacy of the estate system. The estate tradition of social distance between the various strata has also survived.

At the same time, the victorious bourgeois class sets personal qualifications up against the prestige conferred by descent, and gives precedence to economic criteria of social status. In this manner a synthetic scale is set up, which includes in one single scale the level of wealth expenditure, educational level, occupation, and descent. Thus a simple economic gradation is synthesised with the traditions of an estate hierarchy. As a result of this synthesis, which is facilitated by the economic conditioning of non-economic factors of social prestige, two different but largely correlated criteria contribute to the evaluation of the style of life. On the one side, style of life is measured by the level of expenditure: that style which gives evidence of greater wealth is higher. On the other, estate traditions play an important part in evaluating the social level: that style of life which is associated with the traditions of the higher estate is higher.

This then in my view is the origin of a synthetic gradation, a gradation which we encounter in the social consciousness of

---

[1] F. Antal, *Florentine Painting and its Social Background*, Kegan Paul, London, 1947, p. 49.

[2] Cf. Ossowska, *op. cit.*, Ch. X.

various social milieux in the world of yesterday and today. In some social milieux, the synthesis is closer to the conceptions of the estate hierarchy. In others, it is closer to a simple grada-tion. An example of a social milieu in which estate-gradations appear to have been predominant was that of Warsaw high society before the first World War or the Latin American milieux which Beals describes, contrasting them in this respect with the United States. Others have drawn a similar contrast between England and the United States, but the former contrast is incom-parably more striking.

'The middle-class family', writes Beals, 'with two cars and no servants, the banker who washes windows in preparation for his wife's tea party, the professor in overalls wielding a shovel in his garden – all are incomprehensible in Latin America . . . there are certain manual activi-ties which may *never* be engaged in even for recreation, certain imple-ments which must *never* be touched.'[1]

In more highly industrialised countries, the situation is dif-ferent, especially among the workers. Here the social stratifica-tion is conceived above all from the viewpoint of an economic gradation; an instance of this is provided by the surveys carried out by the Swedish Gallup Institute in 1943 to which I have already referred.

*The Synthetic Evaluation and the Degree of Consistency of Simpler Evaluations*

In a synthetic scale, as I said earlier, the various factors that determine overall social status may compensate for each other within certain limits; for instance, lack of education or humble birth may be offset by a high income, while modest means may be counterbalanced by high social status.

The qualification 'within certain limits' requires special atten-tion. The offsetting of some factors involved in social prestige by others leads without hindrance to synthetic evaluations when the discrepancies between the positions of the individual in the various simple scales are not too great. When these discrepancies are considerable, a synthetic evaluation may be replaced by the interplay and combination of simpler evaluations, and, if there is no consistency between them, the individual may find himself in

[1] Beals, *op. cit.*, p. 339.

a marginal position. If, for instance, the discrepancy between an individual's economic position and the level of his education is too great in relation to the approved norms in a particular milieu then the individual deviates from the personality pattern accepted in a given social class; this affects both his social status and his psychological attitudes, whether he has a high income and a glaring lack of elementary education or holds two university degrees but earns barely enough to keep himself alive.

To put it another way, from the viewpoint of a synthetic gradation the social status of an individual does not only depend on each separate factor involved in the evaluation; the degree of consistency among these prestige-conferring factors is also a factor in assessing social status.

In 1952, G. H. Lenski carried out a study in Detroit which has considerable methodological interest. This study was concerned with the following problem: to what extent does what I call a consistent or inconsistent social status (Lenski's 'high or low status crystallization') influence the political tendencies of the individual concerned and also his class identification.[1] One of Lenski's conclusions was that status inconsistency favours the development of radical views. This conclusion is in accord with intuitive knowledge based on various previous observations. For instance, it was noted in Poland long ago that the leaders of the workers' movement in the second half of the nineteenth century were frequently recruited from the declassed *szlachta*.[2] But these are problems which are only incidentally connected with our present subject-matter.

## Objective Criteria and Non-Objective Scales

There is a sociological study by Alain Touraine, entitled *Rapport sur la préparation en France de l'enquête internationale sur la stratification et la mobilité sociale* and published by the International Sociological Association in connexion with a project for

[1] *op. cit., A.S.R.,* 1954.

[2] The Polish historian, Stanislaw Ploski, maintains that this phenomenon was already clearly noticeable at the beginning of the 1860's. He provided me with this interesting piece of information. After the arrests of workers in the Evans factory in Warsaw, and the later arrests of other Warsaw workers and craftsmen in 1862, 65 persons appeared in court. This was one of the major cases before the Rising of 1863 and over 20 (one-third of the accused in the dock) were of noble (*szlachta*) origin.

international studies of social stratification.[1] In a brief introduction the author differentiates between the concept of social
'class' and the concept of 'stratum'. In his conception of classes
he follows the Marxian tradition, defining them as 'groups determined by their place in the social process of production'[2] and at
the same time as elements in a system of opposites (*éléments d'un
système contradictoire*). Also following Marx, he assumes that class
consciousness (*une conscience de classe pure, c'est à dire entièrement
antagonistique*) is formed in political struggles. He defines a stratum
(*le strate*) as 'the total of individuals who are comparable from the
viewpoint of one or several objective criteria of classification'
(*critères objectives de classement*).[3]

Touraine's system of strata corresponds to our scheme of
gradation, just as does Center's concept of stratification. The
author's suggestion is that the concept of the social ladder is
predominant over class consciousness in occupational groups
whose role in the social process of production is more complicated and less distinct. He suggests, in fact, that members
of the liberal professions, merchants and craftsmen are less
ready to adopt the concept of class, which in Touraine's interpretation is close to the Marxian conception, and are more prone
to accept the concept of a system of strata based on criteria of
wealth.

In this case, the system of strata can be reduced to a simple
economic gradation. But as the author writes elsewhere of an
ordering of strata 'from the viewpoint of one or several objective
criteria of classification' it is worth while emphasizing a certain
important difference between a simple gradation and a synthetic
gradation which Touraine fails to consider. A scale which is fixed
not on the basis of one, but on the basis of the interplay and combination of two or more objective criteria, is not an objective
scale if the criteria are concerned with characteristics which are
not commensurable. In the evaluation of social status educational
levels and income levels are such incommensurable characteristics; as originality of ideas and technical performance are such
characteristics in the evaluation of a work of art.

[1] *Association Internationale de Sociologie*, Congrès de Liège, 1953, 'Communications'
Vol. I.
[2] *Ibid.*, p. 1.
[3] *Ibid.*, p. 25.

In hierarchies of this sort – where social status is determined by a comparison of incommensurable factors – for instance, when origin is compensated for by higher income or when a lower economic status is offset by high occupational status or better education – we are concerned with a phenomenon frequently encountered in social life. This is the establishing of some kind of gradation on the basis of intuitive comparison and intuitive summation of values that are incomparable in terms of any other common measure but that resulting from the predilections of the evaluating individual.

This does not mean that we are concerned in this case with individual predilections. Synthetic evaluations of social statuses resulting from the comparison of incommensurable values become social facts characteristic of the particular milieux of those who make the assessments. This is because they are an expression of the 'social consciousness'; that is to say, they have become more or less agreed upon in the consciousness of those members of a particular milieu who are exposed to each other's influence. It is the members of the milieu who achieve the synthesis, but the resulting synthesis varies in different milieux. This affects *inter alia* the role which is directly played by the economic factor in this synthetic gradation or, in American sociological language, the degree to which 'social class' approximates to 'economic class'. In different social classes the particular criteria of class affiliation carry a different weight.

The synthetic gradation which is specific to the 'social consciousness' of a given milieu appears not only in the direct statements of its members, but also in the system of social relationships, in the social isolation of 'high society', and in the activities of individuals who aspire to social advancement or who are endeavouring to maintain their existing social status.

In this manner, the synthetic scale gives us some information about the environment in which the evaluations are made and about its values-system. In some cases such an environment may indeed be co-extensive with the sum total of the groups that are being compared. Warner introduces some complicated calculations to establish a synthetic gradation for the population of Jonesville from the viewpoint of Jonesville's population. In such cases, the image of social stratification is synthetic in yet another sense. For in addition to the synthesis of the factors involved in the gradation which is made by each of these various groups the investigator has produced his own 'synthesis' of the viewpoints of the different classes. This happens when the investigator, instead of relating the image of the social structure to the different milieux, is anxious to present this structure as resulting from the conceptions which he has found in the different milieux. If his material consists, not of the results of surveys directly concerned with class membership but of enquiries into individual and group behaviour in their mutual relations, his results will probably differ less from the conceptions held in the various classes than it will if the investigator makes use only of the survey findings.

By contrast with a simple gradation, a synthetic gradation cannot be applied to groups whose political rights have been legally established (legalized) because it does not provide an objective ranking scale. The influence of a synthetic gradation in the formation of social relations become apparent where the decisive role is played by generally-agreed and intuitive evaluations of incommensurable factors, and not where the letter of the law is decisive.

I have discussed the concept of synthetic gradation at some length, because it is one of the two ways of conceiving class structure that are most widespread in our time. The Marxian triad – capitalist, petit bourgeois, proletarian – is confronted on the other side of the ideological front by other ways of thinking about social matters, ways which in this particular case are expressed by the synthetic gradation of classes. Here we find, not capitalists, the petit bourgeoisie and the proletariat, but the upper, middle and lower classes which are the object of so many American sociological studies.

My purpose here has been to stress the point that when a scheme of gradation is applied in studies of social stratification, objective relations can be justifiably presented only in terms of a simple gradation. When social status is determined by a synthetic ranking scale, studies of social stratification will be concerned with social consciousness. This indeed is the way in which American investigations into the system of social classes are as a rule concerned. For instance, Centers describes 'class', by contrast with 'stratum', as a psychological phenomenon in the fullest sense of the term.[1] For Warner and Lunt, social classes are cate-

[1] *Op. cit.*, p. 27.

gories according to which the members of a society rank themselves and others in superior and inferior social positions.

In spite of this fundamental difference between a simple and a synthetic gradation, and despite the fact that amongst the factors that determine the synthetic ranking scale we are not concerned only with characteristics which lend themselves to gradation, a synthetic gradation can be included in the same general scheme of gradation which we outlined earlier and which comprises a simple gradation. For here too people are ranked with respect to their inherent characteristics according to a relation which is conceived as asymmetrical and transitive.[1] In this case the system of social classes is fixed by an ordering relation and not by a relation of dependence.

---

[1] A transitive relation is such a relation R that if it holds between *a* and *b* and also between *b* and *c*, it holds between *a* and *c* (e.g. 'older than').

# Chapter IV

## FUNCTIONAL CONCEPTIONS

*Distinct Functions and Reciprocal Relationships*

IN ADDITION to the dichotomic scheme and the scheme of gradation there is a third way of conceiving social structure – which may be called the functional scheme. In this conception a society is divided into a certain number of classes differing in accordance with the functions which they fulfil in social life. Here one is concerned with functions more general than those which distinguish various occupations in a society with a well-differentiated division of labour. The distinctiveness of functions entails definite relationships between classes. By virtue of their distinct functions the classes may be mutually essential to one another, in the same way as different occupational groups are necessary to one another. Because of their separate functions the interests of the various classes may also be incompatible. In either case, whether the emphasis is on harmony in the performance of tasks or on conflict of interests, we may in the functional scheme discern a network of reciprocal relationships.

In dividing up those tasks whose performance is of importance for the whole society, Aristotle distinguished between warriors and those citizens who manage the affairs of state. He also divided the working population into land cultivators and artisans and distinguished between those who perform essential work in private service and those who perform such work in the public service (this last division distinguished private slaves from other categories of the working population). Peter Skarga[1], following the Church's interpretation of mediaeval society, declared that 'mankind is divided into three estates: those who pray

---

[1] The Polish Jesuit and political writer (1536–1612).

those who defend the country and those who toil – the priests, the knightly order and the working people'. A similar justification used to be given for the three-estate structure of French society which lasted until the French Revolution, although this division had ceased to be one of function and had become one of privilege by the 17th and 18th centuries.

As modern capitalist society began to take shape, Adam Smith introduced another trichotomy based on economic criteria in place of the traditional estates, the priests, the knights and the labourers. In the 19th century this division achieved wide popularity. The three basic classes into which Smith divided a modern society consisted of proprietors of land, proprietors of stock, and labourers. These classes were differentiated by clearly defined functions in the national economy, and by their role in the processes of production. But Adam Smith, being an economist, found his starting-point in differences in the source of income. He therefore formulated this division of society into classes (still using the old term 'order') as a division into the class of those who lived by the rent of land, those who lived by the profits of stock and those whose source of livelihood was the wages of labour.[1]

A division of classes so interpreted may give the impression of not being concerned with relationships between people, unlike all the conceptions we have considered so far, but with the relations of people to things. One has only to read Adam Smith's further arguments, however to realize that the differences between the sources of income are the result of the differences on the functions which people perform in the life of the society, and that differences in the source of income in their turn entail differences of interests and are connected with the system of privileges and discriminations. Adam Smith does not use the terminology to which the works of Marx and his followers have accustomed us (such terms as 'class interest' or 'class struggle') but he does deal with the problems which are associated with these terms, laying stress on the relationships of dependence between various classes. He considers the conflict of interests between people belonging to these different groups,[2] speaks of the disadvantages suffered by those who receive their wages from labour and

[1] *An Enquiry into the Nature and Causes of the Wealth of Nations*, Vol. I, London, 1931 edition, pp. 41–8 and 57–60.
[2] *Ibid.*, p. 58.

describes the various symptoms of the phenomenon which we call the class struggle and which Smith called 'offensive or defensive combinations'. In accordance with the 18th-century ideas which were later taken over by Marx and Engels, Smith drew a contrast between relationships in primitive society and those in societies with a class structure. There were no social classes until the three basic functions in economic life were differentiated.

'In that original state of things which precedes both the appropriation of land and the accumulation of stock, the whole produce of labour belongs to the labourer. He has neither landlord nor master to share with him.'[1]

The conception of social structure in which social classes are distinguished according to the source of their income and the differentiation of their interests was to be taken up in America at the end of the 18th century in the course of discussions on the role of political parties. James Madison, the future president of the United States,[2] followed Adam Smith in basing his class differentiation on the unequal division of property and the different sources of income, and thus also on differences of interests, on which Madison laid the greatest stress. In place of Smith's neat triad, (the rent of land, the profits of stock, the wages of labour), Madison adopted a larger number of classes with conflicting interests, the number of these classes being limited by any requirements of social design. By comparison with Adam Smith's conception, this conception weakened the distinctness of the class structure. On the other hand, Madison described the social classes in terms close to Marxian language. He brought out the manifold consequences of a functional differentiation of social roles in economic processes, thereby stressing the objective significance of this particular aspect of the social structure. Madison noted the class character of political parties, the reflexion of class interests in legislation, the conditioning of standpoints and sentiments by a class interest, which was too strong to be counteracted by religious and moral considerations. Indeed, Madison's observations on this point lack only the term 'super-structure'.

'But the most common and durable source of factions has been the various and unequal distribution of property. Those who hold and

[1] *Ibid.*, p. 57.

[2] Born 1751, died 1836.

those who are without property have ever formed distinct interests in society. Those who are creditors, and those who are debtors, fall under a like discrimination. A landed interest, a manufacturing interest, a mercantile interest, a moneyed interest, with many lesser interests, grow up of necessity in civilized nations, and divide them into different classes, actuated by different sentiments and views.'[1]

It is difficult to be certain whether we would be in accord with Madison's intentions in reducing the multi-divisional perception of class structure which emerges from his writings to a functional scheme. For Madison does not give his views on the social role of the various classes but merely discusses their interests and the influence of these interests on politics and legislation. In any case one can say that the principles of the dichotomic scheme and of the functional scheme are involved in his observations about social class.

In the United States of today, class structure is, as we have seen, most frequently conceived in terms of a scheme of gradation, but we do in certain instances encounter a functional scheme. Adam Smith's traditional triad here assumes the form of the 'three major functional groups in American society'.[2] These are the farmers, 'labour' and 'business'. In the multi-divisional schemes we are dealing not only with farmers and the working class or 'labour' but also with the categories of 'entrepreneurs', 'professional employees', 'managerial employees', 'white-collar workers' and so on. One even comes across a category called 'architects of ideology', meaning those who shape opinion and ideas.[3] This latter category, which includes writers, artists, scholars, teachers and journalists, has a narrower scope than the Polish concept of the intelligentsia, but it is distinguished by virtue of those functions which the Poles regard as the most significant and characteristic functions of an intelligentsia as a distinct social group. For our 'intelligentsia clubs', so popular in Poland since the end of 1955, are intended precisely for those people whose duty it is to 'shape opinion and ideas'.

[1] J. Madison, 'To the People of the State of New York', *The Federalist*, No. 10 (1787) ed. P. L. Ford, New York, 1893.
[2] D. Bell, 'America's Un-Marxist Revolution', in the collective publication, *Class, Status and Power*, p. 169. Cf. also R. S. Lynd and H. M. Lynd, Middletown, New York, 1929, p. 22.
[3] Corey, *The Middle Class, loc. cit.*, p. 278.

## The Functional Scheme and the Class Hierarchy

The classes which, in the dichotomic scheme, are differentiated according to the relation of one-sided dependence, can also be related by a mutual interdependence. And, conversely, in the functional scheme, which is a scheme of mutual interdependence, one can also discern relations of one-sided dependence between the classes. This is done by Adam Smith when he speaks, for instance, of the combinations entered into by capitalists against the workers. A system of social classes differentiated on the basis of functional criteria can form into a hierarchy of classes, since certain categories of social roles are in various respects privileged in relation to others. But when we see a hierarchy of classes in a functional scheme, this is not related to any gradation which could be regarded as uniform. Class C may be superior to class B in a different way and for different reasons than class B in relation to class A. In Adam Smith's scheme the relationship between the class of those who draw their income from the rent of land and those who live by profit differs from that between the class of those who live by profit and the class of those who live by wages. Yet a third kind of relationship exists between the first and the last of these classes (excluding the great landowners, who not only perform their own functions but also those of the capitalist class in their organization of hired labour). The case of the estate-hierarchy of nobility, bourgeoisie and peasantry is a similar one. The bourgeoisie is not intermediate between the nobility and peasantry in the same sense in which the middle class is intermediate between the upper and the lower classes in the scheme of class gradation. We cannot say that the nobility stands in the same relation to the bourgeoisie as the bourgeoisie does to the peasantry, unless we cease to be interested in the specific social roles in an estate structure and look for an aspect of the estate structure that could be conceived in terms of a scheme of gradation (a gradation of power or a gradation of social prestige).

As the society that is emancipated from estate restrictions approximates more closely to the ideal type of capitalist society, the nature of the wealth possessed ceases to be significant for the determining of an individual's position. An owner of moveable capital may become a landowner and *vice versa*. Apart from temporary market fluctuations, the main things that hinder such changes are psychological factors such as traditions, habits, personal inclinations, life aspirations or professional qualifications.

For this reason the particular source of income in a capitalist society does not provide a permanent basis for a hierarchical system of the property-owning classes. As we know, conflicts sometimes arise between these classes to decide who shall dominate political and economic life. We may cite as instances the disputes over customs tariffs in England or the clashes of interest between industry and agriculture in the United States or between light and heavy industry in Hitler's Germany. But the relationship between the various property-owning classes in the hierarchies of privileged status is a matter of circumstance. The only enduring hierarchical relation within such a class-system is the relation between the property-owning and propertyless classes. But when we examine this relation, the functional scheme is reduced to a dichotomic scheme. For this reason Adam Smith's scheme has in the course of time lost its appeal. And even if one comes across it sometimes in statements made in the United States in slightly different terms, (farmers, business and labour) the criteria of the division are not so distinct as they used to be.

*Functions and Privileges in Estate Hierarchies*

A distinct hierarchy of social class roles, linked with separate functions in social life but not directly determined by the amount of income or property, may be found in a society where privileges have a basis other than in riches, where wealth does not open the door to the performance of all functions, but where there exists a group monopoly over certain types of property and occupation. Such a society may be found in a system of closed classes, that is to say in an estate or caste system.

The members of the various castes or – in cases where the original basic castes have been broken down into a large number of endogamic groups[1] – the members of the various clusters of castes carry out definite functions in the life of the society as a whole. Similarly, the members of the various estates perform

---

[1] In the India of Vedic times the population was divided into four castes: Brahmins, Kshatryas (the knightly caste) Vaishyas and Shudras. Later the Shudras broke up into ritually 'clean' and 'unclean' Shudras. In later times there were more than 200 castes in India, which were split into still smaller endogamic sub-castes.

definite functions. With these functions are connected definite caste or estate privileges or forms of discrimination. For a long time such structures were conceived in terms of the functional scheme; this presented the vertical order of strata simultaneously and thus in terms of a scheme constructed both on symmetrical relations of mutual dependence and on asymmetrical relations of graded privileges. Antal summarized the conception of St. Thomas Aquinas as follows:

'The orders of society, and their various kinds of work, are ordained by God; each order has its special *raison d'être*, each individual must remain in the station to which it has pleased God to call him – he must stay in his own order and his own work.'[1]

In those structures, however, where the individual's membership of a particular social stratum is institutionally fixed, and in particular where this membership is determined by descent, the function which is performed is not the original determinant. It is not the function of the individual in group life that determines his caste or estate affiliation but the affiliation of the individual to a caste or estate that determines his function. This is the meaning of the second part of the above statement from Aquinas.

The same applies in a certain sense even to the clerical order in Roman Catholic societies, although the Catholic priesthood cannot there be hereditary. The blood-tie is here replaced by sacramental rites conferring on the individual life-long personal qualifications analogous to those which the Brahmin receives at his birth.

In caste and estate structures we are concerned not only with the institutionalization of group membership but also with the fact that the entire hierarchy of strata is based on legal or religious sanctions. The various strata have their place in the social structure directly assigned by secular ecclesiastical laws, reinforced by tradition and often by a special ritual of prestige. In principle an inferior caste is not inferior because its members perform inferior functions, but simply because it consists of people of inferior descent who for this reason perform inferior functions. This is the theoretical background, or rather, the ideological explanation of the caste system. But this theory conflicts with the growing conviction amongst the under-privileged

[1] Quoted by F. Antal, *Florentine Painting and its Social Background*, Kegan Paul, 1947, p. 39.

castes that the inferior function degrades those who perform it. Thus in recent years we have seen the revolt of the untouchable castes in India, the refusal to perform actions that pollute, such as the removal of carrion and waste matter. This refusal is based on the conviction that to sever the connexion with polluting activities will remove the degrading stigma from these castes.[1] The esteemed social functions of the Brahmins and the Kshatryas had the same significance, for without them the myth of descent would be insufficient to sustain the power of the caste hierarchy in the social consciousness.

## Economic Classes in an Estate Structure

Estates and castes are basically closed groups and membership of them is determined by descent or through magical rituals with indestructible social consequences. For this reason, the enrichment or impoverishment of individuals, and the resulting differentiation of class positions which are not legally fixed, are all accomplished without infringing estate barriers. Here one must overlook such exceptions as the purchase of titles of nobility by wealthy bourgeois, which in France from the 14th century onwards furnished a considerable portion of the royal revenues.

Since the economic consequences of estate privileges and restrictions do not prevent the formation of a class stratification within the various estates, a scheme of simple economic gradation in an estate or caste society may take various forms and the dichotomic scheme which we came across in the mediaeval accounts may not apply only to relations between the various estates, such as the nobility and the peasantry. For instance, the excerpt from the Communist Manifesto cited earlier is concerned with such class distinctions within a single estate (that of the bourgeoisie).[2]

It depends on the way of perceiving such a complicated estate-class social structure whether these distinctions and gradations of social classes in the images of the estate or caste society are extended to the whole society or confined within the boundaries of particular estates. The question is whether the estate system overlaps the system of economic classes in the social consciousness or

---

[1] Cf. R. Mukerjee and colleagues, *Inter-Caste Tensions*, mimeograph, University of Lucknow, India, 1951.

[2] See p. 31 above.

whether the formation of distinct class structures is perceived as limited to particular estates. In the first instance, we are concerned with something in the nature of a synthetic gradation based on incommensurable criteria such as descent, estate privileges and property. This would make it possible to compare the social status of a poor noble or squire and a wealthy burgher within the same complicated system of stratification. In the second instance, we see the poor noble at the bottom of one ladder and the rich burgher at the top of another, without a synthetic scale which would take into account both the individual's place on the ladder and the relation between the two ladders.

Interesting examples of the intersection of an estate and a class structure in relationships between estates are to be found in a study by Stefan Czarnowski,[1] particularly in regard to the awareness of common interests felt by the magnates (top nobility) and the wealthiest burghers. But the gulf separating the nobility from the non-nobility was so great from the ideological standpoint of the nobility that it prevented the emergence of the perception of a synthetic gradation within the social structure, in which classes based on economic criteria might cut across the boundaries of estates in the Polish Commonwealth of that time. The situation was different elsewhere, as for instance in the country of Samuel Pepys.

The social structure of the United States, and particularly of the South, with its sharp separation of institutions and social contacts along the lines of racial division, is also not usually conceived of as an intersection of the caste structure (black and white) with a class structure but as the result of combining two different systems of class-gradation (the class-system of the white group and the analogous class-system of the Negroes) in a two-caste system. In such a system wealth cannot compensate for descent. The social status of the wealthy Negro and that of the poor white are not comparable according to a single synthetic ranking scale. In the New England state of Connecticut, Hollingshead, a post-war student of social structure, went even further.[2] Endeavouring to look at the society of New Haven through the eyes of the local

[1] 'La réaction catholique en Pologne à la fin du XVIe et au début du XVIIe siècle', Stefan Czarnowski, *La Pologne au VII-e Congrès International des Sciences Historiques*, 1933.
[2] A. B. Hollingshead: *op. cit.*

population, he was inclined to see several parallel class-structures, each within the limits of an ethnic group, such as the Anglo-Saxon, Negro, Polish, Italian and Irish groups. The vertical order of these groups, each with its own system of institutions and organizations, with the Anglo-Saxons at the top and the Negroes at the bottom, might appear to resemble a caste hierarchy, although the ethnic groups in New Haven are not separated by common law, as is the case with the white and black castes in the Southern States.

One may risk the generalization that in societies with a complex structure, where the estate or caste-hierarchy does not coincide with the economic gradation, there will at the highest levels of the economic gradation be a tendency to conceive of the social structure from the viewpoint of a synthetic gradation. It will be conceived as an intersection of a caste or estate-system with an economic class gradation, and not as the co-existence of separate systems of economic gradation, each within a different estate or caste. Men of great wealth are inclined to attach greater importance to economic power than to estate privileges. Hence the facility with which the wealthiest members of the bourgeoisie and the economic élite of the aristocracy can come to an understanding, and hence the frequent manifestations of class solidarity over estate barriers which could be observed in societies such as those of pre-Revolutionary France or sixteenth-century Poland. This contrasts with the relations which generally prevailed between the nobility of moderate wealth and the moderately wealthy bourgeoisie. On the lowest level of the economic gradation one may also expect to find a tendency to accentuate the economic divisions extending through the entire social structure. Poverty affords favourable circumstances for perceiving social relations in economic terms and for minimizing political or social privileges as compared with the possession of wealth.

In the lowest economic stratum of the higher estates of castes, however, we find an opposite tendency too. Here estate or caste affiliation may be stressed as a fundamental qualification, so as to shield the impoverished from a feeling of social degradation. Hence the behaviour of those daughters of impoverished squires who 'herd their cattle not in a peasant's sabots but wearing shoes and who reap the harvest or even spin in gloves'. Hence too the heavy emphasis on their caste superiority in relation to Negroes which is often found amongst poor whites, particularly amongst the newly-declassed poor whites in the United States. Nevertheless, the results of a number of recent investigations support the thesis that racial prejudice, which destroys the image of a synthetic gradation within the whole society, is displayed most strongly amongst the American lower-middle class.[1]

[1] Cf. Dollard, J. *Caste and Class in a Southern Town*, New Haven 1937; G. Myrdal, *An American Dilemma*, New York, 1944.

# Chapter V

## THE MARXIAN SYNTHESIS

*The Doctrine of Marx in the History of Social Ideas*

THE MID-NINETEENTH century saw the birth and development of the comprehensive theoretical system of Marx and Engels. This system aimed at achieving a synthesis of the problems of sociology, economics, philosophy and history, in which general propositions of the type encountered in natural science would provide the foundation for concrete historical conceptions, and in which the most abstract principles and metaphysical assumptions would provide a starting-point for deductions leading to practical conclusions in the sphere of political and economic activity.

If one measures the significance of a theoretical work by the scope of its social consequences, one must regard the Marxian system as one of unusual importance. For a century, writers and men of action fighting for a new order have been reared on the ideas contained in this system. These ideas have shaped the social consciousness of the most active sections of the working class in Europe and beyond and have provided the justification and theoretical foundation for many social programmes. They have constituted the sources of energy for the revolutionary movement by spreading the belief that the realization of revolutionary aims and designs is guaranteed by incontrovertible laws of history.

But the works of Marx and Engels have yet another significance, in that they achieved a great synthesis in the history of thought. There has been a general tendency in the Marxist camp to over-estimate the originality of particular views propounded by

Marx. In almost all his fundamental basic ideas the author of *Das Kapital* had his forerunners. Lenin aptly defined the three sources of the Marxist system: German philosophy, English political economy and French utopian socialism. But these three do not by any means exhaust the cultural heritage which found expression in the works of such absorptive writers. To outline the history of Marx's predecessors, one would also have to mention writers whose work was not directly known to Marx, such as Babeuf, who in a letter to Chades Germain of 28 July, 1795, on the eve of the *Plebeian Manifesto*, formulated *inter alia* the idea of *la loi barbare dictée par les capitaux*.

The originality of the founders of Marxism and the epoch-making role of Marxist theory consist in the bold deduction of far-reaching consequences from assumed ideas; on the development of ideas of varying origin into a coherent system; on the association of theoretical conceptions with a programme of action, with an analysis of historical events and with a vision of the future; and on the achievement of a great synthesis of various trends in theoretical thought and ideological currents. In this regard, the writings of Marx form some sort of immense lens which concentrates the rays coming from different directions, and which is sensitive both to the heritage of past generations and to the creative resources of modern science.

Since Lenin's death we have been wont to associate Marxism not with the metaphor of a lens but with that of an optical device which, as far as post-Marxian theory is concerned, lets through only the rays coming from one direction. This is one of the reasons why as a rule both the followers of Marx and his opponents fail to appreciate the whole varied range of the connexions which link his doctrines with the general history of European thought.

These connexions in Marx's theory appear quite clearly in his analysis of the concept of social structure, that is to say in his concept of class. In choosing a heading for this chapter I had in mind this particular synthesis of the various ways of conceiving social structure, rather than the overall synthesis of the Marxian *Weltanschaung*.

## The Concept of Social Class in Marxian Doctrine

The concept of social class is something more than one of the fundamental concepts of Marxian doctrine. It has in a certain sense become the symbol of his whole doctrine and of the political programme that is derived from it. This concept is expressed in the terms 'class standpoint' and 'class point of view', which in Marxist circles used until recently to be synonymous with 'Marxist standpoint' or 'Marxist point of view'. In this sense 'class standpoint' simply meant the opposite of 'bourgeois standpoint'.

According to Engels,[1] Marx effected a revolutionary change in the whole conception of world history. For Marx, so Engels maintained, had proved that 'the whole of previous history is a history of class struggles, that in all the simple and complicated political struggles the only thing at issue has been the social and political rule of social classes'.

The concept of social class is also linked with what Engels in the same article calls the second great discovery of Marx, to which he attaches so much importance in the history of science – the clarification of the relationship that prevails between capital and labour. Finally, it may be said that the concept of social class is bound up with the entire Marxian conception of culture as the superstructure of class interests.

The role of the class concept in Marxian doctrine is so immense that it is astonishing not to find a definition of this concept, which they use so constantly, anywhere in the works of either Marx or Engels. One might regard it as an undefined concept of which the meaning is explained contextually. But in fact one has only to compare the various passages in which the concept of social class is used by either writer to realize that the term 'class' has for them a variable denotation: that is, that it refers to groups differentiated in various ways within a more inclusive category, such as the category of social groups with common economic interests, or the category of groups whose members share economic conditions that are identical in a certain respect. The sharing of permanent economic interests is a particularly important characteristic of social classes in Marxian doctrine, and for this reason it has been easy to overlook the fact that although it is, in the Marxian view, a *necessary condition* it does not constitute a *sufficient condition* for a valid definition of social class.

Marx left the problem of producing a definition of the concept of social class until much later. The manuscript of the third

[1] ME, Vol. II, p. 149; the quotation comes from F. Engels, *Karl Marx*.

volume of his *magnum opus*, *Das Kapital*, breaks off dramatically at the moment when Marx was about to answer the question: 'What constitutes a class?' We do not know what answer he would have given if death had not interrupted his work. Nor do we know whether he would have attempted to explain the discrepancies in his earlier statements.

After the death of Marx, Engels did not take up the question which the manuscript of *Das Kapital* left unanswered. Lenin's later definition, which has been popularized by Marxist text-books and encyclopaedias, links two different formulations but fails to explain how we are to regard them. Does the author see them as two equivalent definitions and does he link them in order to give a fuller characteristic of the designate of the concept of class? Or is the conjunction of the two formulations essential because the characteristics given in one of them are not necessarily conjoint to the characteristic given in the second? Independently of this, such metaphorical expressions as the 'place in the historically determined system of social production' may be variously interpreted and Lenin's definition is sufficiently loose to be applicable to all the shades of meaning found in the term 'class' as used by Marx and Engels.[1] Bucharin's definition,[2] which is also intended to reflect the Marxian conception of social class, affords room for even wider possibilities of interpretation, and it is only Bucharin's classification of social classes that enables one to grasp the denotation assigned by the author to the concept of social class.[3]

In using the concept of class based on economic criteria, Marx sometimes restricts the scope of this concept by introducing psychological criteria. An aggregate of people which satisfies the economic criteria of a social class becomes a class in the full mean-

[1] 'Classes are large groups of people which differ from each other by the place they occupy in a historically determined system of social production, by their relation (in most cases fixed and formulated in law) to the means of production, by their role in the social organization of labour and, consequently, by the dimensions and method of acquiring the share of social wealth of which they dispose. Classes are groups of people one of which can appropriate the labour of another owing to the different places they occupy in a definite system of social economy.' (V.I. Lenin, *A Great Beginning*, in *The Essentials of Lenin* in Two Volumes, London, Lawrence & Wishart, 1947, p. 492.)

[2] N. Bucharin, *Historical Materialism, A System of Sociology*, London, 1926, p. 267 (English translation).

[3] *Ibid.* pp. 282–4.

ing of this term only when its members are linked by the tie of class consciousness, by the consciousness of common interests, and by the psychological bond that arises out of common class antagonisms.[1] Marx is aware of the ambiguity and makes a terminological distinction between *Klasse an sich* and *Klasse für sich*, but he does not in general make much further use of these more narrowly defined concepts.

Marx sometimes uses a different term to denote a class which is not a class in the fullest sense because it lacks psychological bonds. For instance, he sometimes uses the term 'stratum'; on other occasions he avoids using a more general term and confines himself to the name of a specified group such as the 'small peasantry'. At times he may even call certain classes which are conscious of their class interests 'fractions' of a more inclusive class. In the case of capitalists and landowners, for instance, Marx sometimes sees them as two separate classes, at others as two fractions of a single class, the bourgeoisie.

All these discrepant uses of the term 'class' were probably the less important for Marx because, according to his theory, further social development would render them obsolete. This was to result from the growth of the social consciousness and from the predicted disappearance of the difference between the *Klasse an sich* and the *Klasse für sich* as well as from the progressive process of class polarization in the social structure.

The matter can however be put in a different way. We may take it that Marx, instead of providing a definition of social class which would make it possible to fix the scope of this concept, is giving

---

[1] Cf. the following passages:

'The separate individuals form a class in so far as they have to carry on a common battle against another class.' (K. Marx and F. Engels, *The German Ideology* (The Marxist-Leninist Library, Volume XVII, London, Lawrence & Wishart, 1940, pp. 48–49). 'The organization of the proletarians into a class, and consequently into a political party.' ('Manifesto of the Communist Party', ME ,Vol. I, p. 41.) 'In so far as millions of families live under economic conditions of existence that separate their mode of life, their interests and their culture from those of the other classes, and put them in hostile opposition to the latter, they form a class. In so far as there is merely a local interconnection among these small-holding peasants, and the identity of their interests begets no community, no national bond and no political organization among them, they do not form a class. They are consequently incapable of enforcing their class interest.' (ME, Vol. I, p. 303; quotation from K. Marx), Bonaparte represented the most numerous class of the French society at that time, the small-holding (*Parzellen*) peasants' (ME, Vol. I, p. 302; quotation from 'The Eighteenth Brumaire of Loui Bonaparte').

the model of a social class, the ideal type which is to be fully realized in the future, in the last stage of the development of the capitalist system. In the period in which Marx wrote, the industrial proletariat of Western Europe was approximating to the ideal type of a social class. Other social groups separated on the basis of economic criteria could be called classes only to a greater or lesser extent, and could approximate to the ideal type only in some respects. Hence endeavours to apprehend them by means of conceptual categories with sharply-drawn boundaries of application must lead to confusion.

However that may be, one should, when considering the Marxian conception of class structure, remember that the component elements of this structure are confined to those groups which Marx calls 'classes' when contrasting them with 'strata', in which ' the identity of their interests (those of the members of a "stratum") begets no unity, no national union and no political organization'.

As we shall see below, the Marxian concept of social class involves certain conceptual complications which are more than a matter of terminology.

## Interpretations of Class Structure in Marxian Conceptions

It has already been said that the works of Marx and Engels constitute a sort of lens which focuses the manifold trends in European thought. So far as the problems discussed in previous chapters are concerned, all three schemes of social structure which were described there are to be found in Marx's conceptions, as well as a new mode, peculiar to himself, of conceiving the class system derived from the intersection of three dichotomic divisions.

## The Basic Dichotomy

Marx and Engels are above all the inheritors of the dichotomic perceptions found in folklore and of the militant ideology of popular revolutions. Reading their works, one never loses sight of the age-old conflict between the oppressing classes and the oppressed classes. I have already mentioned the dichotomic perceptions of the drama of history that appear in the Communist

Manifesto and in Engels' work written three years earlier. The reader will recall the two-fold way of conceiving human relations within the social structure in terms of a dichotomic division: the manifold polar division of the various oppressor and oppressed classes in earlier societies gives way to a single all-inclusive dichotomy. According to the forecast of the Communist Manifesto, the capitalist society was to achieve this dichotomy in full in the penultimate act of the drama, in the period that precedes the catastrophe. In approximating to such a dichotomy, the social structure of the capitalist world would then be nearing its end.

According to the founders of Marxian doctrine, the society in which they lived was characterized by a tendency to develop in the direction indicated above. In this society Marx discerned 'the inevitable destruction of the middle bourgeois classes and of the so-called peasant estate'.[1] In Engels' version, the era marked the accomplishment of 'the division of society into a small, excessively rich class and a large, propertyless class of wage-workers'.[2] The workers' rising in Paris on 22 June, 1848, was regarded by Marx as 'the first great battle . . . between the two classes that split modern society . . . the war of labour and capital'.[3]

## Two Conceptions of the Intermediate Classes

Marx the revolutionary and Marx the dramatist of history developed a dichotomic conception of a class society. Marx the sociologist was compelled in his analysis of contemporary societies to infringe the sharpness of the dichotomic division by introducing intermediate classes. He could not overlook the 'mass of the nation . . . standing between the proletariat and the bourgeoisie'.[4] These intermediate classes were a very important element in the pictures of his own era given us by Marx in his historical studies. Sometimes he speaks of 'intermediate strata' when giving a narrower definition of a social class. Elsewhere the

[1] ME, Vol. 1, p. 75; quotation from K. Marx, *Wage, Labour and Capital.*
[2] ME, Vol. 1, p. 73; quotation from F. Engel's Introduction to Marx's *Wage, Labour and Capital.*
[3] ME, Vol. 1, pp. 147, 148; quotations from K. Marx, *The Class Struggles in France, 1848–1850.*
[4] *Ibid.* p. 137.

term 'middle estate' appears, although in this context it does not denote an institutionalized group such as the French *tiers état*.

There is such a variety of social statuses and economic positions in these intermediate classes that it is difficult to confine them within a uniform scheme. The term 'intermediate classes' suggests a scheme of gradation. And in fact one sometimes finds in Marx's writings the conception of the intermediate classes as groupings of individuals occupying an intermediate position in the economic gradation in respect of their relation to the means of production, or to the variety of their social roles and sources of income. For instance, in the *Address of the Central Community to the Communist League*, written by Marx and Engels in 1850, the petit bourgeoisie includes the small capitalists, whose interests conflict with those of the industrialists. And again, in his *The Civil War in France*, Marx refers to the 'liberal German middle class, with its professors, its capitalists, its aldermen and its penmen,'.[1] Here he conceives of the middle class in the sense in which the term is used in England or the United States. A capitalist – that is to say an owner of the means of production – may belong to one class or another depending on the amount of capital he owns. One should however bear in mind that Marx is not thinking here of 'high society' nor of rows and columns in statistical tables. For him the amount of capital owned by an individual is associated with separate class interests.

It was not, however, this conception of an intermediate class that was incorporated in the set of basic concepts in the Marxian analysis of the capitalist society. In constructing his theoretical system, Marx set up the foundation for another conception of the class which occupies the intermediate position between the class of capitalists and the proletariat. This conception was not in fact formulated in its final form by either Marx or his pupils. It is nevertheless related to the scheme of class structure of the capitalist society that is characteristic for Marx and Marxism, a scheme in which three social classes correspond to three kinds of relations to the means of production.

In this scheme the intermediate class, which Marx usually calls the 'petit bourgeoisie' regardless of whether reference is being made to urban or rural dwellers, is determined by the simul-

[1] ME, Vol. 1, p. 447: quotation from the *Second Address of the General Council of the International Working Men's Association on the Franco-Russian War.*

76

taneous application of two criteria. Each of these criteria taken separately forms the basis for a dichotomic division of social classes, although in a different way. One criterion is the ownership of the means of production. This is a criterion which, in a dichotomic scheme, divides society into propertied and propertyless classes. The second criterion is work, which, however, in contradistinction to Saint-Simon's conception, does not include the higher managerial functions in capitalist enterprises. We have come across this second criterion in the dichotomic scheme as well. It divides society into working classes and idle classes. In this conception, the intermediate class consists of those who belong to both the overlapping categories; those who possess their own means of production and themselves make use of them.

Marxism applies still another version of this trichotomous division, a version which is usually not differentiated from the former one. In it the first criterion of division (the ownership of the means of production) remains the same. On the other hand, the second criterion is not work but the fact of not employing hired labour. In this version, the intermediate class is more narrowly defined than in the earlier one. It does not include all those working people who possess their own means of production but only those who work on their own account without employing hired labour. According to this version, a wealthy farmer who employs two or three regular hired labourers, or who has smallholders working for him in exchange for an advance in cash or kind, is included in the class of rural capitalists. In the first version the petit bourgeoisie includes two strata; those who work in their own work-shops and employ hired labour, and those who do not employ such labour. Sociologically speaking, the first version is more suited to describe some conditions, the second more suited to others; thus it depends on various circumstances which need not be discussed here. The combination of the two versions gives two functionally differentiated intermediate classes, as the diagram on the next page shows.

From the viewpoint of the Marxian assumptions concerned with the tendencies of development in capitalism, the position of the petit bourgeoisie, which is intermediate between the two basic classes, is sometimes interpreted in yet another way. The petit bourgeoisie is said to belong to the propertied class so far as present conditions are concerned, to the proletariat with regard

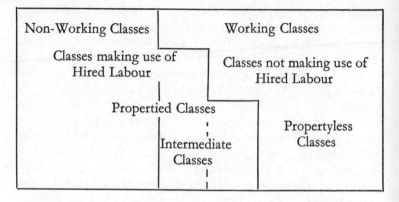

to its future prospects. Thus not only the craftsman but also the small-holder are potential proletarians.[1]

There is also an economic gradation that corresponds to this trichotomous scheme. The capitalist class is that class which owns large-scale means of production or at least sufficient to make possible the employment of hired labour; the petit bourgeoisie consists of those who dispose of the means of production on a modest scale; while the proletariat is in principle the class that owns no means of production whatsoever. In this functional scheme, however, it is not the degree of wealth that determines the boundaries between classes but the social roles, namely their relation to the means of production, work and their relation to the hiring of labour. In the scheme of gradation referred to earlier, on the other hand, the middle class could also include *rentiers*, the owners of small industrial establishments and other capitalists with property not exceeding the limits of 'moderate wealth'.

A strict observance of functional economic criteria in distinguishing the three classes – capitalists, petit bourgeoisie, and proletariat – leads, however, to conflicts with sociological criteria. For instance, an engineer would in his capacity as hired labour in a capitalistic establishment have to be included amongst the proletariat, as would a doctor employed in a private sanatorium. As we know, Marx associated the concept of the proletariat with the

---

[1] Cf. Engels: *The Peasant Question in France and Germany*, ME, Vol, I. pp. 384, 395. Bucharin, in developing Marx's theory of social classes, differentiates the category of classes intermediate between the two basic classes in a different way than is done in our scheme; he distinguishes intermediate classes, transition classes and classes of mixed types. (*op. cit.*, pp. 283–4).

conception of a fundamental dichotomy. The proletarian is a man who is unprotected from the extremes of exploitation by any special qualifications which would prevent him from being replaced by another worker with equal physical strength. According to Marx's intentions, this criterion would exclude the engineer or doctor from the class of the proletariat.

Moreover, according to the Marxian assumption that a class is united by the common interests of its members in great social conflicts, yet another factor may help to correct a scheme based on 'relations to the means of production'. For instance, the salary of the engineer employed by the capitalist includes a portion of the 'surplus value' produced by the workers and appropriated by the capitalist.

In summing up our discussion of this classical Marxian scheme of social roles in relation to the various ways of conceiving the social structure which were discussed earlier, we may consider it as an overlapping of a dichotomic view and a scheme of gradation. In this conception the intermediate class is determined by the boundaries of the two basic and antagonistic classes. It is separated from the others by virtue of the fact that these two basic classes are divided against each other, not by one single criterion, but by two or three criteria to which correspond class-groupings of varying extensions. The intermediate class is made up of people who are connected with each of the two basic classes but in differing respects. This connexion exists both in the logical sense (characteristics which enter into the definition of two basic classes) and in the sociological sense. At the same time, as I have already pointed out, the petit bourgeoisie, as determined by its peculiar 'relations to the means of production', occupies a central position in the trichotomous economic gradation (the extent of ownership of the means of production).

## A Trichotomous Functional Scheme without an Intermediate Class

With Marx the revolutionary, the dichotomic conception of social structure is dominant. With Marx the theorist, we sometimes have to deal not only with the trichotomous scheme with a middle class between the two opposing classes but also with a scheme which is inherited from bourgeois economics. This is the trichotomous functional scheme of Adam Smith. This scheme appears rarely in the works of Marx and Engels,[1] but its importance is increased by the fact that it is the starting-point of the last chapter of the third volume of *Das Kapital,* the chapter which is devoted exclusively to an analysis of classes in modern society. This uncompleted chapter, entitled 'Classes', opens with the words:

'The owners merely of labour-power, owners of capital, and land-owners, whose respective sources of income are wages, profit and ground-rent, in other words, wage-labourers, capitalists and land-owners, constitute then three big classes of modern society based upon the capitalist mode of production'.[2]

And a little further on, when he is dealing with the question 'What constitutes a class?' Marx again takes precisely this conception of the social structure as his starting-point.

In the dichotomic conception and in the trichotomous Marxian conception which I have discussed earlier the emphasis is placed on human relationships. In Smith's conception, on the other hand, the viewpoint of an economist rather than of a sociologist is dominant. The main stress falls on the relations of people to things. Clear economic categories, that is criteria concerned with relationships to things, leave no place in the social structure for the intermediate classes which a sociologist cannot overlook. In Adam Smith's scheme those who own their own means of production and yet work themselves do not form a separate class but belong to two or three classes simultaneously.

'It sometimes happens, indeed, that a single independent workman has stock sufficient both to purchase the materials of his work and to maintain himself till it be completed. He is both master and workman, and enjoys the whole produce of his own labour, or the whole value which it adds to the materials upon which it is bestowed. It includes what are usually two distinct revenues, belonging to two distinct persons, the profits of stock, and the wages of labour.'[3]

[1] Cf. *Ludwig Feuerbach and the End of Classical German Philosophy* (ME, Vol. II, p. 356); Marx's letter to Engels of April 30, 1868 (K. Marx and F. Engels, *Selected Correspondence*, Moscow, Foreign Languages Publishing House, n.d., pp. 245–50).

[2] K. Marx, *Capital*, Vol. III, Moscow Foreign Languages Publishing House, 1959, p. 862.

[3] *op. cit.*, Vol. I, Everyman's Library, p. 58.

Marx considers this point in the third volume of *Das Kapital*, and even accords it conditional approval.[1]

Thus we find two different trichotomous schemes of social structure in Marx, to both of which may be applied the definition of class as a group determined by the relation to the means of production. In the first case (capitalists, petit bourgeoisie, proletariat), the various classes have correspondingly *various relationships to the means of production*. In the second case (landowners, owners of capital and those who own nothing but their own labour), the classes are determined by the *relation to the various means of production*, the capacity to work being regarded here as a category of the means of production.

## A Multi-Divisional Structure

A functional scheme can contain more than three classes, as we saw with Madison. In Marx's writings a direct formulation which would conceive of social structure in terms of such a multi-divisional scheme is nowhere to be found. But if we bring together statements made in various works we find that even an image of this kind can be derived from his works. In his *German Ideology* we find the bourgeoisie and the class of the large industrialists set against each other as classes of different and in a certain respect even opposite social functions; for the interests of the bourgeoisie are contained within national boundaries, while the large industrialists form a cosmopolitan class on an international scale.[2] In his *Class Struggles in France* Marx shows us how the class interests of the French financial aristocracy clash with those of the industrial bourgeoisie.[3] Marx attributes to the financial

[1] 'When an independent labourer – let us take a small farmer, since all three forms of revenue may here be applied – works for himself and sells his own product, he is first considered as his own employer (capitalist), who makes use of himself as a labourer, and second as his own landlord, who makes use of himself as his own tenant. To himself as wage-worker he pays wages, to himself as capitalist he gives the profit, and to himself as landlord he pays rent. Assuming the capitalist mode of production and the relations corresponding to it to be the general basis of society, this subsumption is correct, in so far as it is not thanks to his labour, but to his ownership of the means of production ( . . . ) that he is in a position to appropriate his own surplus labour.' *Capital*, Vol. III, Lawrence & Wishart, London, 1960, p. 853.

[2] K. Marx and F. Engels, *The German Ideology*, Lawrence and Wishart, 1939, pp. 24–26.

[3] 'The mania to get rich not by production, but by pocketing the already available wealth of others'. *The Class Struggles in France 1848–1850*, ME, Vol. I, pp. 128–29.

aristocracy the 'desire to enrich themselves not by production but by cleverly appropriating to themselves riches that already exist', and calls them ironically 'the *lumpenproletariat* on the heights of bourgeois society'.[1] Apart from these two rival classes, Marx mentions the petit bourgeoisie which is removed from political power. A year or so later, in his description of the same society in *The Eighteenth Brumaire*, Marx once again shifts the line dividing the bourgeoisie into two antagonistic factions. This antagonism, for which the ideological superstructure was the conflict between Orleanists and Legitimists, is seen as the outcome of the competition between capital and ownership of land.[2] These factions, based on the ownership of different types of wealth, are the two basic classes from Adam Smith's scheme.

If we now take the class differentiation of the rural population, as it is presented for instance by Engels in the introduction to his work *The Peasant Wars in Germany*,[3] and if we do not overlook the *lumpenproletariat* – which is not a 'class' according to the Marxian definition but a 'stratum' – 'a mass sharply differentiated from the industrial proletariat'[4] – a stratum which can play a specific role in social movements – we obtain an image in which the capitalist society is functionally differentiated into seven, eight or even nine classes or strata.

## The Overlapping of Viewpoints

In his character of revolutionary, economist and sociologist, Marx inherited all three basic types of conceiving the class structure which are encountered in the history of European thought. These are the dichotomic scheme, the scheme of gradation and the functional scheme. At the same time he introduced a characteristic way of conceiving this structure, by intersecting two or three dichotomic divisions. It is this latter way that has come to be regarded as the classic Marxian scheme, although Marx does not employ it when he is discussing the concept of class in the last pages of his greatest work.

We have noted in Marx's writings two versions of this classic

[1] *The Class Struggles in France 1848–1850*, ME, Vol. I, p. 131.
[2] K. Marx, *The Eighteenth Brumaire of Louis Bonaparte*, ME, Vol. I, pp. 247–53.
[3] F. Engels, Prefatory Note to *The Peasant War in Germany*, ME, Vol. I, pp. 584–86.
[4] *The Class Struggles in France 1848–1850*, ME, Vol. I, p. 142.

Marxian scheme, and also an explicit formulation of Adam Smith's trichotomous functional scheme; there is also an implied multi-class version of a functional scheme which recalls that of Madison. Thus it may be maintained that the works of Marx and Engels contain at least six different ways of conceiving the structure of contemporary capitalist societies. The definition of a social class which refers to the relations to the means of production is just as applicable to the classic Marxian scheme as it is to the schemes of Adam Smith and of Madison.

The schemes may differ, but this does not involve contradictory assumptions. The dichotomic aspect of the Marxian theory of classes indicates the direction in which capitalist societies will develop; seen in this perspective the multi-divisional schemes are intended to refer to transitory phenomena. But even without a reference to trends of development the Smithian scheme cited in the third volume of *Das Kapital* and elsewhere need not run counter to the basic dichotomy. It is sufficient to group land-owners and owners of capital in a single more inclusive 'superior' category of 'propertied classes' and to set them against 'those who own nothing but their own labour' as the 'propertyless class'. The trichotomous scheme of gradation may be reconciled with the dichotomic conception by treating the middle class as a grouping resulting from overlapping class extensions or as one determined by the boundaries of the two opposite classes.

We may still seek other explanations. In the Marxian image of capitalist society the dichotomy refers to the classes that participate in capitalist production, which, it should be noted, is not the only form of production in existing capitalist societies. The dichotomy is a basic scheme for the Marxian model of a capitalist society, with its two large classes which appear '*à l'interieur de l'atelier capitaliste*', as Labriola puts it. But this dichotomous class-division of capitalist society is not inconsistent with the existence of other social groups, so long as one accepts the view that other forms of relations of production and their corresponding classes have survived from the past within this society. The dichotomic scheme is intended to characterise capitalist society with regard to its dominant and peculiar form of relations of production, while the multi-divisional scheme reflects the actual social structure.[1]

[1] 'Dire que le capitalisme est caracterisé par l'organisation autoritaire de la fabrique et la division en classes – capitalistes et salariés – qui en découle, ce n'est

Adam Smith's scheme brings out other problems than does the Marxian scheme based on two or three criteria of division. The petit bourgeoisie which occupies such an important position in the Marxian sociological analysis of the French society of that time is not sufficiently important from the viewpoint of certain economic problems for Adam Smith to differentiate it in his functional scheme. Adam Smith does not, however, overlook the existence of the petit bourgeoisie: he describes them as people who, on the basis of certain economic criteria, belong simultaneously to two or three of the classes differentiated in his image of the social structure. This is not incompatible with the classic Marxian scheme, in which the petit bourgeoisie, as an intermediate class, is connected with the proletariat by one criterion, and with the capitalist class by a second.

The founders of Marxian doctrine found this image of the social structure convenient for certain theoretical and practical purposes, while another might serve better for other purposes.

## Two Categories of the Class Struggle

It must not be forgotten that the use of the same terms in describing reality in its different aspects and in formulating generalizations made from different viewpoints can lead to misunderstandings. It is easy to overlook the fact that the concept of the class struggle, the basic concept for Marxian doctrine, comprises two different categories of historical process. The first includes liberation struggles within the framework of the perennial conflict between the oppressing classes and the oppressed classes; the second includes struggles between classes competing for power in a society with a multi-divisional structure. It is not often perceived that the class struggles referred to in the first chapter of the *Communist Manifesto* are social conflicts of a kind different

---

pas nier qu'avec le capitalisme survivent d'autres régimes économiques. ( . . . Si Marx) s'occupait des deux grandes classes qui existent à l'intérieur de l'atelier capitaliste, il ne pouvait pour cela supprimer d'un trait de sa plume autoritaire petite bourgeoisie, groupes professionnels et autres métiers inclassables'. (Arturo Labriola: *Karl Marx – L'économiste – Le socialiste,* Paris 1909, p. 185–86). Sorel points out that Marx frequently confuses logical constructions with his descriptions of actual phenomena, and conjectures that Marx did not always realize the abstract character of his theory of classes.

from those mentioned by Engels in his introduction to a new posthumous edition of Marx's *Class Struggles in France*.

In the *Communist Manifesto* we read:

'The history of all hitherto-existing society is the history of class struggles. Freeman and slave, patrician and plebeian, lord and serf, guildmaster and journeyman, in a word, oppressor and oppressed, stood in constant opposition to one another, carried on an uninter-rupted, now hidden, now open fight.'

In Engels' introduction, on the other hand, we find quite another picture of the class struggle:

'All revolutions up to the present day have resulted in the displacement of one definite class rule by another; but all ruling classes up to now have been only small minorities in relation to the ruled mass of the people . . . the common form of all these revolutions was that they were minority revolutions. Even when the majority took part, it did so – whether willingly or not – only in the service of a minority.'[1]

I have cited these two well-known passages to show that both those who, while regarding the class struggle as the driving force of history, treat the history of class struggles at times as if it consisted exclusively of the conflict between an oppressed majority and a minority of exploiters and at other times as if it consisted exclusively of conflicts between minority classes competing for power could appeal to the example of the classics of Marxism.

It is as well to realize this point, for this duality is linked with tendencies to still greater simplification in presenting historical events. An instance of this may be found in the tendency to regard the so-called 'premature liberation movements', such as the peasants' or workers' insurrections in the periods preceding the full triumph of the bourgeoisie, as if they had no other significance in history than that conferred on them by their participation in the struggles between classes occupying superior positions in the social structure and competing for power. One of the leading Marxists of contemporary France, Garaudy, ascribes a reactionary role to the French Communists of the 18th century, on the grounds that their activities weakened the offensive strength of

---

[1] ME, Vol. I, pp. 113–14; the quotation comes from F. Engels' Introduction to Karl Marx's *The Class Struggles in France, 1848–1850*.

the bourgeoisie in its struggle with the feudal lords.[1] Writing forty years earlier, Jaurés would appear to have given a similar evaluation of the conspiracy of Babeuf.

## The Sharpness of Class Divisions and The Class Interpretation of Cultural Phenomena

It would seem that in the very assumption that class struggles are the driving force of history, two different views concerning causal relationships are intertwined.

The first of these views holds that the driving force of history consists of struggles between an oppressed class and an oppressor class. The second maintains that it comes from struggles between classes with different interests. Among Marx's predecessors, the first view recalls Babeuf, the second Madison or Ricardo. In the first case, the basic phenomenon adduced in causal explanations is the appropriation of the 'surplus value' and the oppression of man by man. In the second it is the antagonisms of class interests, antagonisms which are not confined to situations in which the appropriation of the 'surplus value' is involved.

It is true that in his conception of history Marx undoubtedly assumes that the necessary condition for the existence of all class division is the existence of an exploited class and that the dichotomic division of society into exploited and exploiters is the source of all class divisions. And this additional assumption, which emerges even more clearly in Engels' writings, gives precedence to the first of the two views mentioned above. On the other hand, in the concrete historical studies of both Marx and Engels, the second view takes precedence and class struggles are interpreted more broadly.

This elasticity in the interpretation of basic concepts is not unconnected with the practical significance of Marxian doctrine as a weapon of revolution. It is no accident that one can single out several different ways of conceiving social structure in the writings of Marx and Engels. Nor is it accidental that such varied

[1] 'Toute doctrine qui tend alors à diviser le Tiers-Etat en mettant au premier plan le conflits nés de l'inégalité des fortunes, diminue la force offensive de cette classe contre le féodalité et joue par consequent un rôle de frein, un rôle réactionnaire Les utopies socialistes jouent alors ce rôle et n'ont par conséquent qu'un caractère négative et rétrograde'. R. Garaudy, Les source françaises du socialisme scientifique Paris 1949, p. 29.

trends of thought have intermingled in the Marxian theory of social class, including trends flowing from the dichotomic view of society, the heritage of folklore and the revolutionary movements on the one side, and on the other side from the scheme of Adam Smith. For the concept of social class to perform the role which it did in the history of Marxism and during the social changes of the last century, it had to satisfy seemingly contradictory requirements. A synthesis of the different aspects of the class structure was necessary for this doctrine, which sees in the class struggle the driving force of history and the justification for its political programme, which seeks the explanation of all historical processes in class antagonisms, and gives a class interpretation to all cultural phenomena.

Because of its militant programme, this doctrine must emphasize in the strongest possible way the sharpness of class divisions and the asymmetry of relations in the social structure. The scheme of gradation and the dichotomic scheme are constructed in terms of asymmetrical relations. The sharpest class division is achieved by this dichotomic conception, in which the division of two classes is the only division.[1] In the scheme of gradation this sharpness is weakened by the introduction of intermediate classes; and the clarity of class contours is still further blurred as the number of classes in the social structure increases. This is particularly so when the number of social classes is not clearly fixed, and when it is possible to distinguish five or at other times six or eight classes.

The dichotomic view is the most convenient for the tasks which the Marxian doctrine was to carry out, because of the sharpness of the asymmetrical divisions. On the other hand, a large number of social classes is an assumption which is needed for the 'class interpretation' of the complicated processes of history and the whole variety of cultural phenomena. This interpretation, which ascribes a many-sided significance to class divisions and draws all spheres of spiritual life into the orbit of the class struggle, cannot

---

[1] In this context is is worth recalling Sorel's view:
'Les propagandistes socialistes ne peuvent se resoudre à subordonner leur conceptions des classes aux faits, qui nous montrent une excessive complexité de la structure sociale; sans la division dichotomique il leur serait impossible de faire comprendre l'idée revolutionnaire, de même que sans la déscription d'un idéal futur ils ne pourraient faire pénétrer dans les masses la notion de la catastrophe morale. Autre chose est faire de la science sociale et autre chose est former les consciences'. Sorel, *op. cit.*, p. 188.

be confined within a dichotomic structure. If all political or religious struggles are to be interpreted as class struggles, if we are to correlate the various literary and artistic trends with underlying class relations, if we are to look for a reflexion of class interests and class prejudices in moral norms, then we must make use of a greater number of classes than the two basic ones in the *Communist Manifesto*.

# Chapter VI

## THE CLASS-HIERARCHY AND THE SOCIAL-STATUS CONTINUUM

### *The Tendency to Question Class Privileges and Class Boundaries*

IN THE last chapter I endeavoured to explain the linking of different schemes of social structure in the Marxian system as due in part at least to a tendency to lay the maximum emphasis on the all-round significance of class divisions. Yet in probably every country in our modern civilization the ruling classes or groups are characterized by the opposite tendency: the tendency to efface the 'class' nature of the existing social order. The reasons for this are easy to understand. On the one hand there is the impact of the democratic ideology of the bourgeois revolutions of the eighteenth century, whose basic assumptions, variously interpreted, passed into the general heritage of European culture and became the watchwords of progress. On the other hand, the fear of the hostility of the under-privileged works in the same direction.

The tendency to efface the 'class' nature of the social structure is however much older than the French Declaration of the Rights of Man or the American Declaration of Independence. It can be discerned without difficulty in ancient Rome or in the Greek city-states, although naturally only in relations between groups of free citizens.

This tendency can appear in more than one form, but above all two points are involved: (i) the questioning of the conflict of class interests and of the importance of class privileges; (ii) the questioning of the existence of distinct class boundaries in the social structure or in general the questioning of the existence of objective bases for class distinctions. The former point is connected with our analysis of the functional scheme, the latter with our analysis of the scheme of gradation. But a questioning of class boundaries can lead to an interpretation of the class structure which has not yet been considered in this study.

## Interdependence and Equivalent Privileges

Wherever there is a tendency to efface the distinctness of social inequalities – whether this is motivated by a desire to deaden the sensitiveness of the oppressed classes or to appease the conscience of the privileged and reconcile the existing state of affairs with the ideology which they profess – we find in the image of the social structure an inclination to give priority to mutual dependence in inter-class relationships. From this point of view the functional scheme may be distinguished from the schemes of social structure considered in earlier chapters. For this functional scheme suggests that the new dependence is mutual, in contrast to the dichotomic conception which emphasizes the asymmetry of class dependence, or to the scheme of gradation, which is also built up on asymmetrical relationships. In Adam Smith's scheme each of the three basic classes has at its disposal different means of production, but no one class can do without the co-operation of the remaining two – provided of course that the system of ownership remains unchanged.

In Adam Smith's theory of social classes, the mutual dependence was not meant to conceal another aspect of the social structure, as I have already pointed out. The author of *The Wealth of Nations* was aware both of the oppression of the working class and of the class antagonism caused by the conflict of interests – nor did he hide this from his readers. It is not really difficult, however, to find in the history of European thought examples of functional interpretations of class structure that are undoubtedly intended to protect the existing social order.

Aristotle associated the different functions of master and slave with a difference in their natures. He considered that although the master's power worked primarily to the advantage of the master the interests of master and slave were nevertheless concurrent. The master needed the slave's physical strength, while the slave needed somebody who could give him orders.[1] According to a

[1] Aristotle, *Politics*, Book I, Chs. V–VI.

Roman legend Menenius Agrippa, when despatched by the patricians to the camp of the rebellious plebeians in 503 B.C., told them a fable about the parts of the body in revolt against the belly. Thereby he is said to have convinced them that social classes are mutually dependent and essential to one another, and to have induced them to return to the city.

The concept of the mutual dependence of social classes expressed in Agrippa's parable was to find expression over twenty centuries later in the Papal Encyclicals. It was also to assume a scientific form in Spencer's theory of the social organism and in Durkheim's reflexions on 'organic solidarity'.[1]

Agrippa's parable must also have been popular in the Age of Enlightenment, since we meet with a criticism of it both in Morelly[2] and in Mably. The latter added that the plebeians did not in fact allow themselves to be convinced by the cunning Agrippa;[3] he also cited the view of the physiocrats that a well-ordered class society forms a 'perfect whole made up of different parts which are all equally necessary to one another'.

In addition to the fundamental view that different classes are necessary to one another because each performs different social functions, we also sometimes come across attempts to justify the opinion that the privileges associated with certain class functions are only apparent or that they lack any great significance. Whereas St. John Chrysostom regarded the wealthy men as drones living off the labour of the poor, Theodoret of Cyrrhus, his junior by half a century, accepted the dichotomic conception of social structure, but was anxious to see in it a division of functions between classes that were essential to one another and not a polar division into a privileged and an under-privileged class.

'Il faut admirer Dieu', writes Theodoret, 'd'avoir organisé les choses si sagement en donnant les richesses aux uns, l'industrie aux autres'.

Theodoret was convinced that close co-operation between the former and the latter groups is a necessary condition for the

---

[1] E. Durkheim, *De la division du travail social,* Paris 1893.

[2] Morelly, *Code de la Nature,* 1755.

[3] Mably, *Doutes proposés aux philosophes économistes sur l'order naturel et essentiel des sociétés politiques,* Oeuvres completes de l'Abbé de Mably, à Lyon, 1792, Tome XIe, Lettre II, pp. 38–39.

[4] *Ibid.* pp. 39–40.

successful functioning of a society and that the division of functions is just. While the rich men are entitled to the privileges of wealth, still more do the poor enjoy privileges of another kind:

'Les serviteurs ont leur maîtres pour compagnons dans leur besoigne et ne participent nullement aux soucis de leurs maîtres.'[1]

One is struck by the persistence of this type of argument in support of the class system. It shows what a close resemblance there may be between the attitudes of people in similar social situations, even when they are remote from each other in culture and time. For instance, we find an American planter of the era of Franklin Roosevelt, fourteen centuries after Theodoret, maintaining that the planter has become a slave amongst the free Negro labourers:

'We have to worry over the crop, over financing the tenant and everything like that, while he just looks to us to take care of him and hasn't a worry as long as he is fed.'[2]

Again, the view expressed by Clement of Alexandria in the third century A.D. – that class privileges are meaningless because only purity of soul has genuine value – could be heard at meetings of the Oxford Group, well after the Bolshevik Revolution.

The questioning of the value of class privileges is intended to weaken the impression that the lowest classes are oppressed, and thereby to lessen the social significance of the class-hierarchy. This does not, however, affect the reality of the class structure. The questioning of its reality appears in some interpretations of the system of human inter-relations and in connexion with the problem of the criteria of class boundaries.

## The Problem of the Sharpness of Class Boundaries

The meaning of class boundaries can be discussed with reference either to inter-class relations or to the class affiliation of individuals. In the first case, the class boundaries are of interest as a barrier in the relations between members of different classes. In the second, the matter of class boundaries should be considered in both a dynamic and a static sense. In other words, we are here

[1] This and the preceding passage from Theodoret are in French translation and taken from G. Walter's 'Les origines du Communisme', Payot, 1935, pp. 198–9.

[2] Statement quoted by the authors of Deep South, University of Chicago Press, 1941, p. 19.

concerned on the one hand with class boundaries conceived as barriers to the mobility of individuals on the social-status scale, on the other with the sharpness with which the dividing line is drawn between classes.

When the class boundaries are conceived as barriers to inter-class mobility, we can speak of a greater or lesser 'penetrability' of class boundaries. The opposite of this 'penetrability' is 'permanent' membership of a social class. 'Permanence' may be interpreted as the high degree of probability that an individual will remain in his class throughout his life. Class membership that is determined on a lifelong basis for each individual corresponds to ideally rigid class boundaries.

The question of the sharpness of class boundaries introduces a special problem where a scheme of gradation is involved. For the same relationship which determines the gradation of classes can constitute the criterion by which individuals are ranked within each class. By way of example let us take a scheme of simple gradation, in which social class membership is determined by the relative wealth of the individual. In practice, this degree of wealth could be differentiated almost *ad infinitum*, whereas the number of classes based on differences in relative wealth is limited to a small number, sometimes even as few as three ('higher', 'lower' and 'middle', or 'rich', 'poor' and 'moderately well-off').

The question then arises: how can a social-status system that is determined by differences of degree in the possession of a certain characteristic become a system of social classes, if no other criterion of class differentiation is introduced? How can a continuum of social statuses on a vertical scale be broken up by class boundaries?[1]

The establishment of such boundaries can be the result of a convention like that of the timocratic system of Solon or Servius Tullius. When such a convention is enforced, class distance depends on the different privileges and restrictions which are associated with membership of one class or another. It does not depend on the differences of wealth that exist between a citizen whose income amounts to 199 medimns and another who has reached the 200-medimn level and so become a member of the zeugite class in Solon's system. In this instance the income level

---

[1] The term 'continuum' is applied here in the sense used by American sociologists; it does not of course denote continuity in the mathematical sense.

is only a conventional criterion. There is therefore no need to ask why the class boundary is drawn across the scale of wealth at this precise point. This question only arises in situations where class divisions are regarded as divisions which have arisen spontaneously.

There are three characteristics of the system, each of which may be recognized as the structural criterion of the class gradation that breaks up the continuity of the system of social statuses. They are: (i) the fact that barriers to upward social mobility appear statistically at certain levels of the vertical scale[1]; (ii) that the status system shows obvious gaps at certain intervals in the scale; and (iii) that certain segments of the scale show a strong concentration of social statuses.[2]

Using these three criteria, one can establish the classes statistically in a scheme of gradation. The first criterion permits us to ascertain the relative permanency of the placement of individuals in certain segments of the scale. The two other criteria enable us to establish the discontinuities and the irregular distribution of social statuses on this scale.

In respect of the first, dynamic criterion, the class division loses some of its significance when possibilities of social mobility, and particularly of upward mobility, are available on a large scale. In respect of the other two criteria of class stratification, the relationship between the scale of social inequalities and the importance of the stratification may be expressed in the following formulae:

Class stratification will be the sharper: (a) the wider the total range of social inequalities; (b) the narrower the range of social inequalities within the boundaries of each class; (c) the smaller the number of classes; and (d) the greater the distance between the top status in the lower class and the bottom status in the class immediately above it. This is however a function of the three conditions (a, b, c). Thus, for instance, given the same general

---

[1] Cf. Andrzej Miller: *Das Problem der Klassengrenze*, I.S.A., Liège Congress, 1953.

[2] W. L. Warner uses this to justify both the objective value of his synthetic social-status scale and the reality of the division of American society with six classes correlated with various segments of this scale. 'The cases bunch there numerically and tend to accumulate near the centre of the class and drop towards the limits of a class range.' 'A Methodology for the Study of Social Class' in *Social Structure* (ed. Meyer Fortes), Oxford, 1949, p. 16.

scale of inequalities and the same number of classes, the smaller the inequalities within each class the greater will be the differences between the classes.

If we introduce one more condition we can formulate yet a fifth regularity on which the sharpness of class stratification depends: (e) given the same range of the total scale of social inequalities, the sharpness of the class stratification increases with the increased polarization of social statuses on the total scale; that is to say, the greater the ratio of the extreme to the middle positions.

The formulae given here can be regarded in two ways: either as some kind of sociological laws concerning the sharpness of class stratification in the social consciousness, arrived at by observation of collective life and conclusions drawn from very general psychogical assumptions, or else as a partial definition of what is meant by the relative sharpness of class stratification. In the latter case one would interpret the degree of sharpness of the class stratification statistically, as a certain set of characteristics of a status system. In the former case the sharpness of the stratification must be described in another way – by reference to psychological attitudes or to the behaviour of members of the collectivity in social interaction.

I have already pointed out that a dichotomic scheme is the most suitable one for bringing out the sharpness of class divisions. This is connected with the third point of our formula, from which it follows at the same time that to increase the number of classes in the image of the social structure blurs the sharpness of class divisions. In connexion with the fifth relationship which we have just considered, that is to say the formula concerned with polarization, the tendency to weaken the class aspect of the social structure favours the emphasis on the importance of the middle classes, in respect both of their numbers and their role in the social processes in the widest meaning of this term. When the middle class plays the most important role in social life, and when the majority of the nation are members of this middle class, blatant inequalities between the classes at the extremes become less important – a sort of 'deviation from the norm'.

To return to the relationship referred to above under the headings (b) and (d). From the viewpoint of structural criteria, we find that, given the same scale of inequalities in social statuses, the greater the differentiation of social statuses within the various classes and the smaller the distances between classes, the less divided will a society be.

Thus it is possible to reduce the sharpness of the class stratification in a social-status system, not by trying to weaken the picture of social inequalities, but by stressing the continuity in the system. Whereas a functional scheme lends itself to use against the theory of class struggle by virtue of the fact that it blurs the impression of class inequalities, the conception of a continuum of social statuses does away with the classes themselves, without heeding the scale of inequalities. Of course by decreasing the range of this scale we also weaken the class character of the social structure in accordance with condition (*a*). This relationship does not however hold both ways; if the sharpness of class divisions is diminished the range of inequalities is not thereby necessarily reduced.

## Two Conceptions of Classlessness

The image of the capitalistic system found in the works of Marx and Engels, particularly in those of their earlier period, approximates to the ideal type[1] of the class society, in so far at least as it is concerned with the dynamic trends which both authors ascribe to the capitalistic formation. According to this view, on the eve of the coming world revolution, capitalistic society will develop all the characteristics of its class structure to the fullest extent. Full class consciousness will then pervade the whole society, which will be rent asunder by a ruthless struggle.

Directly opposed to the Marxian view of social structure in a class society is the image of a classless and egalitarian society. This conception too is included within the scope of Marxian doctrine. A society of this kind would be the communist society; according to the laws of Marxian dialectics the development of capitalism should lead to this society through its last phase, when the basic characteristics of the class society would be intensified to the utmost.

In these visions of the future we are dealing with two ideal types of social structure at the two extremes of a scale. Both are concerned with the large societies of modern industrial civilization. Between these extremes we can order the various kinds of

[1] 'Ideal type' is here used in Max Weber's sense.

contemporary societies, both capitalist and socialist; but obviously we shall not achieve a uniquely determined rank order because several different criteria of distance from one and the other extreme are involved.

Marx's view of the future communist society is associated so closely with the term 'classless society', and this term has been so coloured by the striving for universal equality, that the phrase used above ('a classless and egalitarian society') might seem redundant. But experience has shown that the term 'classless society' has acquired another meaning than that involved in the Marxian ideal type. The abolition of the class-system can be understood as the wiping-out only of those inequalities which result from class divisions. In this sense the abolition of social classes does not necessarily mean the abolition of the status-hierarchy or of economic inequalities. The liquidation of levels in the social structure does not necessarily involve the destruction of the social ladder. The abolition of the system of class privileges does not entail the abolition of all the privileges whereby individuals differ from one another. The point is – which of these privileges are regarded as not being associated with the class-system.

The conception of the classless society, wherein classlessness by no means presupposes economic egalitarianism, appeared, it would seem, simultaneously with the triumph of the idea of modern democracy founded upon free competition, after the fall of the estate order and the wiping-out of estate privileges (or at least those which were enforced by legal sanctions). This was the interpretation of the structure of France given by the bourgeois writers of the first half of the nineteenth century and by the textbooks of civic education in the Third Republic. Today we meet this conception – the conception of a classless society which economically is not egalitarian – on both sides of the line that divides the world into two camps. And this is the last conception to be considered in our review of the ways of conceiving social structure.

*Equality amongst the Unequal in Estate Orders*

This democratic image of equality amongst the unequal did not however arise for the first time in conjunction with modern bourgeois democracy. We meet this view of the social structure far earlier, but in a narrower domain; we meet it in estate-systems, not with reference to the society as a whole but to the structure of the privileged estate, the structure of the collectivity of full citizens.

In Poland, contrary to everyday practice and even to the statute-book, which singled out within the *szlachta* (nobility) separate classes with considerably differing privileges, the ideology of this estate presented the nobility as a whole or at least the landed nobility (*szlachta osiadta*)[1] as a classless community, although it was not egalitarian economically or in the amount of influence commanded by individuals. This was the meaning of the classic formula 'the gentleman in his croft is the equal of the magnate aloft'[2] and of the other phrases that circulated about equality amongst the *szlachta*. It was also the meaning behind the ban on accepting hereditary titles, in which the Polish nobility (*szlachta*) forestalled the United States. This prohibition was in no way incompatible with the widespread predilection for personal titles and titles taken from a father's office, such as *wojewodzic* (son of a provincial governor) and *podczaszyc* (son of the royal cup-bearer). The form of address 'brother' (*Panie bracie*) was in principle, but only in principle, supposed to be obligatory in relations between all members of the noble fraternity. It was intended to be an eloquent proof of the classlessness of the society of gentry, more eloquent even than the classless American railway-carriage as a sign of equality in Abraham Lincoln's country. Makarewicz describes how the term 'lesser *szlachta*' was inserted in a statute of 1690 relating to hearth-tax, but removed in 1697, with the admission: '*in aequalitae* there is no "lesser" and no "greater".'[3] Diderot and d'Alembert, authors of the *Encyclopaedia*, saw Poland as a country in which extreme serfdom coexisted with

[1] The law dealt both with differences of descent and of property, contrary to the generally accepted view. The following categories of the *szlachta* were recognized: *Bene nati* in contradistinction to those who were ennobled (*scartabelli*), *possessionati* in contradistinction to those who had nothing ('Just as the title of nobility (*szlachectwo*) gives *habilitatem ad possessionem*, so *possessio* gives *legalitatem ad dignitates*' – so ran a passage from the 1578 Constitution), and even in certain cases *bene possessionati* in relation to those who owned little land. The law also took into account the hereditary character of the estate owned by an individual: '*Illi personae, quae . . . habuerint haereditaria ibidem bona*'. J. Makarewicz, *Polskie prawo karne* ('Polish Criminal Law'.) Lwow-Warsaw 1919, pp. 336–40.
[2] '*Szlachcic na zagrodzie równy wojewodzie*.'
[3] *Ibid.* p. 340.

extreme freedom and love of equality – equality within one's own estate.[1]

A similar classless but non-egalitarian society was the community of Athenian citizens as portrayed in Pericles' speech of 431 B.C.[2] This portrait was moreover nearer to reality in various respects than the picture of equality amongst the *szlachta* claimed for Poland in the days of Orzechowski or Pasek,[3] although the adherents of the ideal of the *szlachta* often referred to the Athenian democracy in support of their case. In speaking of the relation between Pericles' speech and the reality, we are of course thinking only of the community of Athenian citizens. For in his praise of the Athenian ideals of freedom and equality, Pericles makes no reference to the existence of slaves and metics, nor to the situation of Athens' allies.

In the next chapter we shall be comparing two contemporary views of society in which social inequalities associated with wide differences in the share of the national income are not interpreted in class categories, and in which rejection of the image of a class-hierarchy goes hand in hand with approval of social inequalities.

---

[1] *En quoi l'histoire de la Pologne est particulièrement intéressante (XII, 1925)*. 'Le comble de l'esclavage et l'excès de la liberté semblent y disputer a qui se détruira. L'égalité entre les nobles est maintenue en Pologne avec beaucoup de soin. Tout ce qui n'est pas noble vit sans considération dans les villes, ou esclave dans les campagnes.'

[2] Thucydides, *Pelopponesian War*, Bk. II.

[3] Both writers presented the ideology of the *szlachta*, Orzechowski in the 16th and Pasek in the 17th century.

# Chapter VII

## NON-EGALITARIAN CLASSLESSNESS –
## SIMILARITIES IN INTERPRETING
## MUTUALLY OPPOSED SYSTEMS

*We believe that further research and writing on social stratification must be prepared for inequality to resurge in many particular guises.*

N. N. FOOTE.

THIS CHAPTER was written in 1953 and 1954. The comparison which it draws between the interpretation of the structure of United States society that is popular in certain American circles and the official interpretation of the structure of the Soviet Union is in general based on material available in 1953 at the latest. Thus it deals with the period in which the social structure of the Soviet Union was relatively stable and provided the model followed by the people's republics, particularly after 1948.

Our discussions do not therefore cover the changes that have occurred in the Soviet Union in recent years, such as the 1956 decision to abolish the fees for secondary and higher education which were introduced in 1940. Nor do they cover the recent changes which have occurred in the United States, particularly since the end of the Korean War, and which were stressed in some papers given at the Third World Congress of Sociology in Amsterdam.[1]

The subject-matter of this chapter has in my opinion a wider significance in that it provides an illustration of the way of con-

[1] See for instance Kurt Mayer's 'Recent Changes in the Class Structure of the United States, and a posssibly over-optimistic paper by Jessie Bernard, 'Class Organisation in an Era of Abundance', in the *Transactions of the Third World Congress, of Sociology*, London, 1956.

ceiving the social structure which was outlined in the foregoing chapter; it also provides a particularly striking example of the application of a similar intepretation of social relationships in mutually opposed systems.

## The Problem of Class Consciousness in the United States

It is generally accepted, not without some grounds, that in the consciousness of the mass of the population the 'class' aspect of one's own society plays a much smaller role in the United States than it does in the capitalist countries of Europe. Such factors as the absence of estate-traditions,[1] the long-drawn-out territorial expansion to the West, the turbulent development of the country's industry, the dizzy careers made by individuals, the opportunities for upward social mobility (so much greater than in Europe), the heterogeneous ethnic composition of the working class, and finally the Negro question – these are the circumstances which have repeatedly been cited as reasons for the differing social attitudes of the American and the European worker, and for the feeble development of the Communist and Socialist movement in the country where private capital is at its most powerful, industrial production greatest and the income-range widest.

This state of affairs is also reflected in American sociology. Except for a small number of sociologists whose attitudes are somewhat 'un-American', American sociology has been isolated from Marxian problems and from Marxian methods of social analysis to a far greater degree than sociology in Western Europe. Just before the Second World War Robert Lynd accused American sociologists of avoiding the term 'class' and the problems connected with it.[2] After the war, this charge was repeated by R. Centers.[3] The Swedish investigator of American social relationships, Gunnar Myrdal, though he drew attention elsewhere and in a different context to the recent interest shown in the problem of social class by the group of investigators led by Professor Lloyd Warner, also wrote in 1944: '. . . American sociology (which

[1] In the legal sense of this term, passing over the *quasi*-estate culture of the Southern States.

[2] *Knowledge for What?* 1939: third edition, Princeton University Press, 1947, p. 227.

[3] 'Perhaps no area of social and psychological research has been so neglected by American scientists as that of class conflict and class consciousness.' *The Psychology of Social Class*, Princeton University Press, 1949, p. 8.

generally must be given the highest ranking in the world) is weak and undeveloped in regard to the problems of social stratification.'[1]

Since these comments were made, studies of the class structure of American society have attained a leading place in the set of problems with which American sociology is concerned. Contributory factors to this development were, it seems to me, the studies of the Negro problem made by Myrdal, Dollard, Doob, the Gardners and others, studies in which the problem of the relation between caste and class could hardly be overlooked. Today there is a growing body of field-research devoted to the class structure of the United States, and particularly of research which has as its common assumption recognition of the psychological criterion of social class, and has as its subject-matter people's opinions about the class-system in which they participate. This sort of approach to social structure is supported by the conviction that in social relationships the only things that matter are those which are immediately predominant in the consciousness of the participants.

As we already know, the American class structure is rather rarely interpreted otherwise than in terms of a scheme of gradation, whether we consider the statements of people representing various American milieux or the findings of field-researchers. Usually a synthetic gradation is involved: the synthesis is achieved in the social consciousness, whereas the theoretician endeavours at best to define the role of the different elements in the synthesis.

## The Stratification of American Society in American Sociology

It is first and foremost within this framework – the scheme of gradation and the psychological criteria of class membership – that discussions of the actual stratification of American society or of its trends of development are carried out amongst American sociologists or political commentators. In discussions of the actual situation, differences of opinion are usually differences in assessing the degree to which certain features of the social structure should be regarded as characteristic of American society. In discussions concerned with trends of development, opposing standpoints clash with each other: destratification or restratification? polarization or the extension of the middle class? Does the class system

[1] *An American Dilemma*, New York, 1944, p. 670.

become more rigid or do rigid class barriers gradually disappear?[1] Nevertheless these opposing standpoints are for the most part not formulated too sharply. In their article, *Patterns of American Stratification as Reflected in Selected Social Science Literature*[2], Paul Hatt and Virginia Ktsanes surveyed the different modes of conceiving the structure of American society found in the work of twenty American social scientists over a quarter-century (1924–1949). They were concerned firstly with the degree of the stratification and distances between classes; secondly with the amount of individual mobility; and thirdly with the emphasis on economic factors in class stratification.

Another subject of discussion in the United States is the importance of the middle class in the American social structure. Until recently it was generally held that the vast majority of people in the United States regard themselves as members of the middle class. This conviction was supported by the Gallup findings of 1939, by the *Fortune* survey and by Cantril's work in 1943.[3] These showed that between 79 and 88 per cent of the population of the areas included in the surveys regarded themselves as belonging to the middle class. Because a certain percentage of respondents did not answer the questions, the percentage of middle class members amongst those who had a definite opinion about their class affiliation was still higher. For instance, 88 per cent of the respondents in the Gallup Institute Poll described themselves as members of the middle class, while only 6 per cent admitted to membership of the upper or lower classes.

Later studies, including the work of Centers, showed that the percentage of persons admitting middle-class membership varies according to the manner in which the questions are formulated. For instance, the figure decreases considerably if, instead of giving the respondent a choice between upper, middle and lower classes an open-ended question is asked. The figure decreases still more if the term 'working class' is included amongst the possible answers.

[1] N. N. Foote, 'Destratification and Restratification'. *A.J.S.* Jan. 1953; A. B Hollingshead: *Trends in Social Stratification A.S.R.* Dec. 1952; G. Sjoberg: *Are Social Classes in America Becoming More Rigid? A.S.R.* Dec. 1951.

[2] *A.S.R.* Dec. 1952.

[3] G. Gallup and S. F. Rae, *The Pulse of Democracy*, New York, 1940; 'The People of the United States – a Self Portrait', *Fortune*, 1940; H. Cantril, 'Identification with Social and Economic Class', *Journ. Abnorm. and Social Psychology*, 1943, cited from Centers, *The Psychology of Social Class*, Princeton University Press, 1949, pp. 30–31 and 237–40.

In the latter case, Centers got a response of 43 per cent for 'middle class' and 51 per cent for 'working class'. In any event, even when these differences are taken into account, the percentage of respondents admitting middle class affiliation clashes sharply with the Marxian prediction of polarization in capitalist societies.

The differing opinions expressed by American writers about the social structure of the United States are concerned not only with the stratification as defined by people's attitudes but also about the objective economic relationships which condition this subjective stratification.[1] Despite all the reservations which I made in Chapter III with regard to the simplification of the American picture of social structure, one should not forget the lively American interest in a simple economic gradation; that is to say, the classification of people according to their income-level and the distinction of various income-groups is a common phenomenon, while terms such as 'five thousand dollar men' or 'twenty-five thousand dollar men' have become everyday currency.

## The Conception of the Classless Society in the United States

In these American discussions of the social structure of the United States we may distinguish an extreme point of view. This is the 'democratic optimism' that questions the whole reality of social classes in American society, thereby shifting the subject of discussion. Here we reach the model of social structure which in the last chapter I called the concept of a classless and inegalitarian society.

In an article published in 1952, G. H. Lenski contrasted two viewpoints held by different American sociologists. He noted that the American social classes on the one hand are regarded as statistical categories which can have only a heuristic significance,[2] on the other as social groups based on a psychological bond.[3] Supporters of the first approach claim that in America the social-status scale from top to bottom closely approximates to a

[1] Cf. J. J. Spenger, 'Changes in Income Distribution and Social Stratification', *A.J.S.*, Nov. 1958.
[2] 'American Social Class: Statistical Strata or Social Group', *A.J.S.* Sept. 1952. Elsewhere we find the same opposition expressed in different terms: namely, that of the 'substantive' and 'classificatory nature of class'. P. Hatt, 'Stratification in the Mass Society', *A.S.R.* April 1950.
[3] Cf. O. Cox: *Caste, Class and Race*, New York, 1948.

continuum[1] and that the concept of class is alien to American society.

The view that the concept of class is alien to American society is based on the conviction that the social attitudes of the average American are formed by the traditional ideology – the so-called American Creed. Is it not true that there are no second or third class compartments in American trains in order that railway installations should not conflict with the principle that there are no classes within the bosom of the great American nation, as William Archer ironically observed at the beginning of this century. For an additional payment one can of course travel in a pullman compartment or a drawing-room, but these are not compartments of a different class. In America, Daumier could not have conceived his lithographs in which the classes on the railway-coaches became symbols of the social structure.

As Ralph Bunche once wrote:

'Every man in the street, white, black, red or yellow, knows that this is the land of the free, the "land of opportunity", the "cradle of liberty", the "home of democracy", that the American flag symbolises the "equality of all men" . . . . .' [2]

One argument adduced to support the view that there are no distinct social classes in America is the way in which those sociologists who do not regard classes as a 'heuristic concept' but consider the social-class system as a real phenomenon in the social consciousness fail to agree as to the number of classes which they differentiate. S. A. Hetzler wrote:

'The Usemovs and Tangent found three distinct social classes, Centers found four, Hollingshead found five and Warner found six. In view of these discrepancies it is quite important that we ascertain whether contemporary society consists of clearly delineated classes or of a composite of statuses and roles arranged loosely on a continuum'.[3]

In the town of Danielson in Connecticut where Lenski conducted his field-research, he found that different people divided the population of Danielson into three, four, five, six and even seven

---

[1] G. C. Homans, *English Villagers of the XIIIth Century*, Harvard University Press, 1941.

[2] Myrdal, *op. cit.*, p. 4.

[3] 'An Investigation of the Distinctiveness of Social Class', *A.S.R.* Oct. 1953, p. 494.

social classes.[1] Lasswell, reporting his findings with regard to the social stratification in a small town in Southern California, stated that the number of social strata mentioned by respondents varied from one (i.e. from a negation of class differentiation) to seven, no one category obtaining more than 17 per cent of the total response. He also pointed to the lack of uniform criteria of class affiliation. These were some of the findings on which he based his conclusion that social strata in Citrus City are not rigorously distinguished by the general population.[2]

The view that there are no classes in American society is frequently encountered in investigations carried out in various American milieux, even when the questionnaire mentions class divisions. 'I don't believe in classes' is a statement expressed by quite a number of American citizens when asked about their class affiliation or inter-class relationships.

As one might have anticipated, this conviction is class-determined, statistically speaking. During an investigation carried out in four districts of Minneapolis, the question was put: 'What social classes do you think there are in Minneapolis and which one of these classes are you in?' In the wealthiest district 19 per cent of respondents replied that there were no social classes at all, whereas only 6 per cent gave the same response in the poorest district.[3] In this type of enquiry it is, of course, difficult to determine how far one is dealing with the repetition of ideological formulae and at what point one is confronted with genuine convictions.

What is in the minds of those who talk of the 'American belief in classlessness'[4] or the American 'tradition that class divisions are un-American'?[5] What is in the minds of those American citizens who say that they 'do not believe in classes'?

From the commentaries on such statements we may deduce that those Americans who believe or would like to believe that

[1] Lenski, op. cit., p. 143
[2] T. E. Lasswell: 'A Study of Social Stratification', A.S.R. June 1954, p. 313. A similar conclusion is suggested in a rather less obvious manner by some material on the attitudes of textile workers in Patterson, New Jersey (cf. J. G. Manis and B. N. Meltzer: 'Attitudes of Textile Workers to Class Structure', A.J.S. June 1954).
[3] N. Gross: 'Social Class Identification in the Urban Community', A.S.R., August 1953, p. 402.
[4] G. Sjoberg (see p. 115, n. 2).
[5] Centers, op. cit., p. 8.

they live in a classless society have in mind the sort of 'classlessness' which we have been considering. This involves an image of society which meets the following conditions:

1. The social and economic status of individuals is not determined by descent; the road to the highest positions is open to all, even though they may not have an equal start.[1]

2. The social-status scale is not broken by any distinct barriers which could transform the continuum-like status order into a gradation of different strata.

3. In accordance with the last condition no definite privileges are attached to the various segments of that scale, nor do any permanent conflicts of interest exist between higher and lower levels of social status.[2]

4. There is no separation or restriction in social contacts between strata.

Civic equality, which is a tenet of the American Creed, is supposed to be based precisely on such classlessness, and not on a levelling-out of social status or income. Each citizen has equal rights and in a certain sense equal opportunities to aspire to lower or higher positions. It is assumed that inequalities of economic or social status are determined not by class affiliation but by personal qualifications, but nobody denies the existence of these inequalities. The great range of achievements is in accordance with the demands of free competition.

Those who rejected this optimistic image of American society did not need to appeal to a Marxian line of argument. In 1889, the American economist Richard Ely scoffed at the dogma of equal opportunities.[3] And at the beginning of this century, William Archer wrote that the lack of class divisions in American trains was just as much a fiction as the classlessness of American society. Forty years later McGuire wrote: 'Social class is a reality of

[1] Parsons maintains that an equal start is impossible in a society in which an 'occupationally-differentiated industrial system and a significantly solidary kinship system' are combined. *The Social System*, Free Press, Glencoe, p. 161.

[2] 'The bourgeoisie are not obviously set apart from the proletariat', wrote M. Rosenberg in a passage contrasting American and European relationships, 'by virtue of owning a car. The differentiation is continuous rather than polar. One man owns a newer or better car than another but this will not induce a feeling of class consciousness in his slightly less fortunate fellow.' 'Perceptual Obstacles to Class Consciousness', *Social Forces*, Oct. 1953.

[3] Cf. R. R. Wohl, 'The Rags to Riches Story', in the collective publication *Class Status and Power*, New York and London, p. 393.

American social stratification if the primary data of contemporary community studies are to have any meaning'.[1] A little earlier Robert Lynd[2] had compared American society to an arena in which elephant and chickens have an equal chance to dance.

The characteristics of the various classes seen as distinct component elements of American society are to be found in the work of various field-researchers who did not confine themselves to questionnaires but followed Lynd's methods.[3] The characteristics of the poor white class in the Southern States as outlined by L. W. Doob remind one of the comparison between social classes and nations made by Disraeli and Engels.[4] Centers spoke of class solidarity and class interests. And in his reference to the great coal strike and President Truman's address to the American people on 24 May, 1946, he speculated whether the class struggle in the United States 'had reached a stage where one could not help but wonder if men were not finding loyalty to a class a bigger and nobler thing than loyalty to a Government'.[5]

## The Contrasting Background

Independently of the degree to which the conception of a classless society actually finds support in the social consciousness and of the sectors of American society in which this occurs, we should remember that in America this image of the social structure is set against the background of the caste-like relationships between white and black, and that this system of caste relationships is marked by characteristics which are a radical negation of all four conditions mentioned earlier. For caste membership and caste-bound social status are decided exclusively by descent; caste-membership is determined for life before a child is born, and the barrier dividing the two classes cannot in principle be crossed. Between white and coloured there is no intermediate status. In the United States, unlike South America, a light-coloured mulatto remains a Negro in his relations with the white caste. There is

[1] McGuire, 'Social Stratification and Mobility Patterns', *A.S.R.*, April 1950.
[2] Lynd, *Knowledge for What?* 1939; 3rd ed., Princeton Univ. Press, 1947, p. 111.
[3] R. S. Lynd and H. M. Lynd: *Middletown*, New York, 1929; *Middletown in Transition*, New York, 1937.
[4] 'Poor Whites: a Frustrated Class', Appendix to J. Dollard, *Caste and Class in a Southern Town*, ed. 1949, pp. 445–484.
[5] Centers: *op. cit.*, p. 7.

caste endogamy and social separation, and the Deep South has strictly enforced institutional separation between the castes. Finally, there are caste privileges, caste etiquette and caste discrimination, masked by the 'Jim Crow' formula of 'separate but equal' but fooling nobody.

This separation of the castes makes it easy to overlook the existence amongst the white population of exclusive clubs which are open only to individuals from the upper social brackets, or of such institutions as the *New York Social Register*. This is an annually-published list of the names of a few hundred distinguished individuals, on which a newcomer can gain a place only if he or she furnishes letters of recommendation from two wives or mothers of persons already listed.[1] Against a background in which caste membership is absolutely determined from birth, the influence of the parents' property and income-level on the class status of their children becomes less apparent, and the frequency with which class status is inherited less striking.

There is one further circumstance which helps Americans to feel this democratic optimism about the social structure of their own country. This is the old tradition of rejecting the class-divisions of Europe, a tradition which goes back as far as the eighteenth century. Americans see these class-divisions chiefly in terms of the relics of feudalism – estate distinctions, aristocratic exclusiveness, the privileges attached to descent from a good family.[2] America banned aristocratic titles in the dawn of its independence, and the good American citizen has been accustomed to compare his country with class-divided Europe, with its dukes, lords, counts and its primitive peasantry, whose representatives he could see in the East and South European immigrant districts of America's cities. And when the son or grandson of such an uneducated immigrant achieved high office in the United States, as a mayor, governor or the owner of a large business, this provided a forceful argument in favour of the fundamental tenets of the American Creed.[3]

---

[1] G. Gorer, *The American People*, New York, 1948, p. 217.

[2] Cf. Myrdal, *op. cit.*, p. 670 and p. 1375.

[3] 'How always have men's hearts beat', wrote Woodrow Wilson in 1913, 'as they saw the coast of America rise to their view. How it has always seemed to them that the dweller there would at last be rid of kings, of privileged classes, and of all those bonds which had kept men depressed and helpless'. *The New Freedom*, New York, 1914.

This dual background – that of the Negro caste and that of the European 'old countries' – has made it easier for good Americans to see the system of social relationships within white society in the United States as a harmonious, dynamic and classless structure: harmonious in respect of the absence of class antagonism and polarising tendencies and also in respect of the number and prestige of the middle strata; dynamic in respect of the degree of mobility of individuals on the rungs of the social ladder.

In all these respects this image of social structure is opposed to the Marxian vision of the capitalist society, the vision of class antagonisms. Nor should we be misled by the use of the term 'dynamic'. The image of American society is dynamic in quite a different sense than is the Marxian theory of classes.

## The Problem of Classlessness in Soviet Society

Looking at the social structure of the United States with eyes accustomed to observe reality through the prism of the class struggle, an East European Marxist is bound to regard American modes of conceiving American social stratification, even those that lay stress on a class hierarchy and on relatively rigid class boundaries, as a sort of mystification aimed at masking the essential class conflicts. The American conception of a classless society must appear absurd to him, for it combines classlessness with capitalism.

Nevertheless, there is one reason why this American conception should not strike a Marxist as absurd. For this extreme, optimistic and democratic view of society, combining classlessness with the maintenance of great differences in the share in the national income, which is contained in a certain version of the American Creed, is by no means alien to the Soviet Union and the People's Democracies in relation to their own societies.

How did the Soviet society of the Stalinist period, described as being 'the second stage of the development of the Soviet state, and which came after the victory of socialism and the transformation of the class structure',[1] appear from the viewpoint of the Communist Creed?

From the phrase just quoted about the transformation of the class structure, it would follow that the Soviet society of this

[1] *Istoricheski materializm* (Historical Materialism), ed. Professor F. B. Konstantinov, Moscow, 1951, pp. 363–402.

period was not classless. And indeed, according to the Stalinist conception, classes do still exist in the Soviet Union, but they are 'non-antagonistic classes', none of them being in a position to appropriate the labour of another class.[1] These classes are the workers and the *kolchoz* peasants – that is to say, the classes whose differentiation is based on the distinction between two forms of socialist property, state property and co-operative property. This differentiation remains in a certain correlation with the differentiation between town and country. The great Soviet Encyclopaedia also links the differentiation with the concept of the two sectors of socialist production. The intelligentsia is mentioned as a third component of Soviet society, but in accordance with Stalin's arguments it is not accorded the name of 'class', but only of 'stratum'.[2]

Seen from the viewpoint of Marx and Lenin, 'non-antagonistic classes' constitute a *contradictio in adiecto*. The authors of 'Historical Materialism' appear to realize this; after citing Lenin's definition of class they write: 'In this sense one can no longer call our society a class-society'.

But the Stalinist conception of 'non-antagonistic classes' breaks away from the concept of class found in Marx and Lenin in favour of a concept that is closer to Adam Smith's idea of classes (different types of property, different sources of income). In relation to the basic concept of social class in Marxist doctrine the qualification 'non-antagonistic' has a modifying and not a specifying function; but in relation to Adam Smith's concept of class it has a specifying function, because Smith acknowledged the existence of class antagonisms, although he did not deduce them from his definition of class.

The conception of 'non-antagonistic classes' arose out of certain requirements of Soviet internal policy. The official recognition of the class of workers and the *kolchoz* peasantry as the only classes still existing in the Soviet Union, distinguished according to objective economic criteria, provided in advance a negative answer to the question whether privileged and under-privileged classes existed in the new social structure. The traditional meaning of the term 'classless society' to which I referred in the preceding

[1] V. I. Lenin, 'A Great Beginning' (1919), from *The Essentials of Lenin*, London, Lawrence & Wishart, 1947, Vol. II, p. 492.
[2] Cf. for instance, Konstantinov, *op. cit.*, p. 402.

chapter was probably also involved. This associated the 'classless society' with the Communist system, which is to be attained only in the future. But a spokesman for the ruling ideology, while acknowledging that classes still exist in Soviet society, will not call it a 'class society' because of the term's old associations: for Soviet society is opposed to such class societies. Therefore it is stated that the fundamental class differences (*korennye klassovye razlicyiha*) have already been altogether overcome in the Soviet Union in consequence of the victory of Socialism.[1]

Quite apart from such terminological complications, the official Soviet image of contemporary Soviet society – an image which is part of the ideological training programme for the whole population – is of a society without class stratification, not only from the Marxist and Leninist viewpoints, but also from the viewpoint derived from the American criteria of the concept of class. In this society there is no exploitation of man by his fellow man, nor are there upper classes and lower classes in the sense in which we encountered them in the American scheme of gradation. The superiority of the working class in relation to the peasantry is, according to Soviet ideology, a superiority of merit and not of privileges. This class occupies the leading place on the common road to Communism and not a higher level in the social structure. The often repeated expression concerning the 'moral and political unity of the Soviet nation' is also a certain way of asserting the classless character of Soviet society, particularly when we consider the Marxist traditions concerned with the ideological superstructure.

This society without class privileges and class antagonisms is not of course an egalitarian society. No Soviet Marxist will deny that the share of individual Soviet citizens in the national income differs considerably. The tendency to *uravnilovka* (equalization or levelling of wages) which characterised the early phase of Soviet society was condemned as incompatible with the principles of Socialism. In the Polish People's Republic, too, President Bierut more than once spoke publicly of progress 'in the direction of putting an end to the so-called *uravnilovka*' and of the need for a further compaign against *uravnilovka*, since private ownership of the means of production had been abolished.

[1] T. Gubariew, *O priodolenii klassovykh razlichii v SSSR* (About the overcoming of class differences in the U.S.S.R.), *Bolshevik*, 1951, No. 5, p.19.

In the Soviet Union economic privileges and discriminations have, in accordance with Soviet doctrine, nothing in common with class divisions. Even large differences of income are not associated with any sort of relationships such as could transform the extensive social-status scale into a class hierarchy. Instead, the individual's place in the scale is determined by his merits.

The idea that a new privileged class may be created as a result of the increasing range of income-differentials is not considered at all. In this respect the Soviet theory of the social structure in the land of socialism differs fundamentally from American conceptions. In judging whether a society is a 'class society' or not, an American is thinking of a gradation of classes based above all, though not exclusively, on income-differences. In the Soviet Union and the People's Democracies this scheme of class structure is not applied at all. Soviet ideology employs only two conceptions of class: the Marxian in relation to other countries, and Adam Smith's conception – in a certain sense – in relation to its own society. The transition from the present socialist system to the classless society is to be accomplished not by a levelling-off of wages but by the abolition of the fundamental differences between towns and countryside and by the merging of the two sectors of the economy – state and *kolchoz* – into one production sector.[1] This conception is linked with the thesis that the present class system in the socialist state is horizontally and not vertically structured.

## Similarities and Dissimilarities

In contrast to the United States, where the American Creed and the conception of 'classlessness' are the subject of analysis and dispute, no variants of the conception of Soviet society were as a rule to be found in Soviet publications before 1954. In comparison with the American optimistic view of American society, the Soviet conception of a harmonious and dynamic society, without antagonistic classes and without *uravilovka*, was formulated in a more definite and radical manner. The similarities are however sufficiently apparent, despite the basic difference over the requirements for human cooperation: there the cult of private enterprise

[1] See the *Great Soviet Encyclopaedia*, under the heading *Classes*.

is stressed, here the subordination of individual activity to social planning on the widest scale.[1]

The Socialist principle 'to each according to his merits' is in harmony with the tenets of the American Creed, which holds that each man is the master of his fate, and that a man's status is fixed by an order of merit.[2] The Socialist principle allows of the conclusion that there are unlimited opportunities for social advancement and social demotion; this is similar to the American concept of 'vertical social mobility'. The arguments directed against *uravnilovka* coincide with the arguments put forward on the other side of the Atlantic by those who justify the necessity for economic inequalities in a democratic society. 'The maximisation of effort in an achievement-oriented society calls for considerable inequality' – wrote Spenger in 1953.[3] This sentence could equally well have been uttered by a statesman in the Soviet Union or the Peoples' Democracies. In the United States this 'optimistic' conception of the system of relationships within the white population has as its background the old countries of Europe and the Negro caste situation within the country. In the Soviet case, the background consists of the relationships that prevailed in pre-revolutionary Russia, and of the capitalist world that today encircles the socialist countries. Stalin wrote:

'The feature that distinguishes Soviet society today from any capitalist society is that it no longer contains antagonistic, hostile classes; that the exploiting classes have been eliminated, while the workers, peasants and intellectuals, who make up Soviet society, live and work in friendly collaboration.'[4]

Communist doctrine assumes that a necessary condition of the development towards a harmonious society – a society in which everyone has an equal start, and there are no antagonistic classes – is the abolition of the private ownership of the means of produc-

[1] For the changes which have been taking place recently in this connexion in American society see W. Friedmann, 'Changes in Property Relations', *Transactions of the Third Sociological Congress in Amsterdam*, vol. II, 1956.

[2] '. . . An order of merit in terms of which men differ with respect to their rights and duties'. J. J. Spenger, 'Changes in Income Distribution and Social Stratification', *A.J.S.*, November, 1953.

[3] *op. cit.*, p. 258.

[4] J. Stalin, 'Report on the Work of the Central Committee to the Eighteenth Congress of the C.P.S.U. (B.)', delivered March 10, 1939, published in J. Stalin, *Problems of Leninism*, Moscow, Foreign Languages Publishing House, 1947, p. 621

tion. But the American Creed does not accept this assumption at all. On the contrary, it regards the system guaranteed by the American Constitution as the one that offers the most favourable conditions for achieving just this kind of society. These incompatible assumptions enable similar conceptions of social structure to be applied in countries with such widely varying economic systems.

In comparing the official conception of Soviet society with the most optimistic and extreme American viewpoints, we should not forget that this similarity refers only to images of the present situation. For both on one side and on the other the trends of development are presented in quite a different manner. The American Creed does not envisage a more perfect system, although it foresees progress in some respects within the present system. The Communist Creed, on the contrary, holds that the socialist society of today is only a stage on the road to a communist society.

This transition to a communist society should, however, according to the prospects outlined by Stalin himself, be achieved not by means of upheavals – as is to be expected of all transitions from one 'formation' to another – but via 'the continuous expansion and perfecting of socialist production on the basis of higher technique'.[1] This means by way of evolution, in the same sort of way in which Americans who, while taking the 'optimistic' view, do not yet regard the American society of today as a 'classless society', visualize the further democratization of the United States.[2] When the future of their own society is concerned, the ruling groups in both the capitalist and the socialist countries always take an evolutionary attitude.

Meanwhile the evolutionary processes are not necessarily proceeding in the predicted direction. The difficulties with which Communist ideology has to cope in connexion with the changes which have taken place in the socialist society are no less than those which the American Creed has encountered in its collision

[1] J. Stalin, *Economic Problems of Socialism in the U.S.S.R.*, Moscow, Foreign Languages Publishing House, 1952, p. 45.

[2] Cf. for instance this passage from C. Sjoberg: 'Although it can hardly be denied that, measured by objective criteria, some kind of class system exists in the United States, historical changes in the social structure may well give substance to the American creed of "classlessness"'. 'Are Social Classes in America Becoming More Rigid?', *A.S.R.*, Dec. 1951, p. 783.

with the American reality. In the United States it was easier to believe in classlessness amongst the white community before the end of the expanding Western frontier with the unlimited possibilities which it offered to enterprising individuals, before the disappearance of the 'no-man's land', and before the great industrial concerns destroyed over large areas the free economic competition that is one of the tenets of the American Creed. And in the Soviet Union it was easier in 1918 to justify the ratios of the differential state wage scale ranging from 100 to 175 than it was in 1950 to justify the ratios of 1 to 40 which prevailed at that time.

## The Marxist Analysis as a Weapon of Struggle

The application of the Marxian scheme of social structure exclusively to the capitalist societies is entirely justified from the the viewpoint of the Marxian theoretical approach, since the Marxian analysis referred solely to the class-system prevailing in a social order where class antagonisms were the result of private ownership of the means of production. Neither Marx nor Engels undertook to analyse the structure of a society in which the means of production were nationalized, and indeed such a society did not exist anywhere at that time. Thus in the Soviet image of Soviet society there is no relinquishing of Marxian assumptions, despite the introduction of the non-Marxian concept of 'non-antagonistic classes'. It would, on the other hand, be possible to say that there has been a relinquishing of Marxian methods of sociological analysis.

Because of the propaganda functions of the social sciences, Marxian methods – and in general all sociological methods that threaten stereotypes and social fictions – are rarely found suitable from the viewpoint of the ruling or privileged groups for the analysis of their own society. On the other hand, they are a useful weapon against outside enemies.

So it is the Soviet Union's opponents in the United States or Western Europe who attempt to use these methods in relation to the Soviet Union. A particularly active part in this is played by Russian émigré intellectuals, who are better acquainted with Marxism and with Russia than are their Western colleagues. In place of the 'non-antagonistic classes' arising from different types of socialist property, they try to detect the formation of a new class structure based on economic privileges and on the exploitation of the labour of others by a privileged class composed of institutionally-established groups: this exploitation being carried out not directly but by means of the state administration and the state treasury, as was done by the court aristocracy in France under the last Bourbons. Those who like to apply Marxian methods to Soviet society in the Stalinist period stress the wide range of wage-scales and the importance of such economic privileges as were not included in the total of monetary rewards. They try to emphasize the tendency to stabilize class differences, citing such features as the great reduction in death duties and the sliding scale for income tax introduced in 1943; the reintroduction of fees for secondary and higher education in 1940, which was confirmed by the amendment of the 121st article of the Stalinist constitution in 1947; the institutionalization of 'class barriers' evidenced by the whole system of rights, subsidies, privileges and so on. In general, they attempt to apply the Marxian theory of the state to the Soviet state, and the Marxian theory of 'opium for the masses' to the ideology propagated in the socialist states.

In the last two chapters I examined the conception of classlessness in the light of certain social tendencies, namely the tendencies to soften the 'class' aspect of the social structure. It emerged that the concept of the classless non-egalitarian society – the concept, not the term – within the frame of differing theories of social class is used for the characterization of one's own society in the leading countries of both the socialist and the capitalist world. In one case this conception is part of the official ideology in which the mass of citizens are reared, while in the other it may rather be said to constitute an extreme expression of a trend which is characteristic of the civic training propagated in that country. In both countries the view of their own society is based on the assumption that even widely ranging shares in the national income are not sufficient to establish social stratification, nor do they necessarily cause either class antagonisms or other symptoms characteristic of a class structure. The differences in economic system prevailing in the two countries are responsible for the fact that this assumption is interpreted in one way on the Western side of the Atlantic and in a different manner in Eastern Europe.

The similarity between the two interpretations of a non-egalitarian social structure is linked with a wider question: that of the causal determination of the various important phenomena of social life which, despite appearances and despite the theoretical simplifications convenient for polemical purposes, do exist in each of the two contemporary opposing forms of economic system. The similarity is also linked with the following threefold problem: in what respects do the institutions and ideologies of the contemporary states which have nationalized the means of production and established a new political order constitute the opposite of the capitalist system; in what respects do they form a continuation of it; and in what respects are the new stages of this new system, now in the process of stabilization, accompanied by a revival of the institutions, relationships, psychological attitudes, and ideas of pre-socialist, socio-economic formations?

# Part II

CONCEPTUAL CONSTRUCTS
AND SOCIAL REALITY

# Chapter VIII

## THE THREE-FOLD DENOTATION OF THE TERM 'SOCIAL CLASS'

### *The Concept and the Term*

IN MY ANALYSIS of the conceptions of class structure, I used the concept of class and the corresponding concept of a class-society regardless of whether or not the term 'class' appeared in the texts examined. I could not in any case have taken the terminological criterion into account since I was also concerned with historical periods in which the term 'social class' did not yet exist.

None the less, when we come to consider modern views on the problems of social structure it is not only the concept of class that is important but the term as well. In the course of the nineteenth and twentieth centuries the term itself has acquired a considerable emotional load and a rich field of associations. It is no longer a matter of indifference which denotata receive their share in this emotional charge. In consequence, the meaning of the term is no mere matter of semantic conventions when one is considering disputes about the concept of class.

For the moment, however, I am concerned with the semantic aspects of this matter. The ambiguity of the term 'class' makes it difficult to find one's bearings among the divergencies between the different viewpoints involved. In the next chapter I shall be considering the problem of the common conceptual content to be found in different conceptions of a class-society. But before that it is as well to realize the relation of the general concept of class to the two concepts with a narrower extension which are as a rule referred to by means of the same term (that is to say, the term of 'class').

In this chapter I shall be dealing with the overlapping of the three denotations of the term 'social class', both with regard to the origin of its threefold nature, which is connected with the social changes of recent centuries, and with regard to the actual requirements of the conceptual apparatus.

## A New Term and a New Reality

The history of the term 'social class' from the second half of the XVIII century onwards is an interesting subject for sociologists. As I have not made any systematic study of it, however, I am confining myself to observations drawn mainly from sources which were consulted for other purposes.

In the *Encyclopaedia* of Diderot and d'Alembert, I could not find the term *classe sociale*, although the word 'class' in the meaning of *social class* is found as early as Spinoza. I am indebted to Professor Leszek Kolakowski for drawing my attention to Proposition XLVI in the third book of the Ethics, which is of interest in this context.[1] In their description of social structure the authors of the *Encyclopaedia* found the terms *état* and *ordre* sufficient for their purpose, *état* being used in reference only to groups with a legal existence, that is to say groups which are organized in a certain way and which have some kind of political representation.

Thus the *Encyclopaedia* could maintain that there were only two estates in Poland (the *szlachta* and the priesthood), while four were noted in Sweden (nobility, priesthood, burghers and peasants) and three in France.[2] Here the term *état* is used, as we can see, in a manner very remote from the general concept of class. Turning to Mably, I was unable to find the term *classe* in his treatise of 1758, *Des droits et des devoirs du citoyen*. He did, however,

---

[1] 'If a man has been affected pleasurably or painfully by anyone of a class or nation different from his own, and if the pleasure of pain has been accompanied by the idea of the said stranger as cause, under the general category of the class or nation: the man will feel love or hatred not only to the individual stranger, but also the whole class or nation whereto he belongs.' (*Prop.* XLVI, R. H. M. Elwes' translation).

[2] 'Le tiers-état', we read in the Encyclopaedia, 'ne commença à se former que sous Louis le Gros, par l'affranchisement des serfs.'

employ the term in his polemic with the physiocrats, written a dozen or more years later, in a sentence referring to the conflict of class interests. In this polemic the term *classe* has a clear economic connotation.[1]

Not many years after the publication of the *Encyclopaedia*, Adam Smith divided society into basic groups, according not to legal but to economic criteria.[2] But he again did not apply the term 'class' to these groups but the term 'order'. We do find the word 'class', in the meaning of a social group, in Smith's works, but it is applied to a more differentiated division. The three basic orders are in their turn divided into 'classes'.[3]

Adam Smith's followers came to apply the term class to his basic groups, and we also find it used occasionally by Madison.[4] At the beginning of the French Revolution Sieyès saw the fundamental social conflict as a struggle between the estates, and used only the latter term in his picture of contemporary social structure and of the homogeneous society of the future.[5]

Some years later, however, Babeuf was writing only of social classes, and was presenting French society as divided by a basic class antagonism. In the new conditions, a new term was essential to underline this antagonism, which Sieyès had not discerned or at least had not mentioned. Babeuf regarded France from the viewpoint of another class than did the Abbé Sieyès. Saint-Simon, however, although in this regard he held the same position as did Sieyès and although his 'industrial class' (*classe industrielle* or *classe travailleuse*) approximately coincides in extension with the third estate, nevertheless applied the term 'class' in his conceptions of social structure, and used a new term, *classe paresseuse*, to

---

[1] 'Qui ne voit pas que nos societiés sont partagées en differentes classes d'hommes, qui, grâce aux propriétés, à leur avarice et à leur vanité, ont toutes des interêts, je ne dis différents, mais contraires?' *Doutes proposes aux philosophes économistes*, Letter VIII. There is a mention of class interests in Letter III and in Letter VIII the author refers to the concept of *classe stérile* employed by the physiocrats. In general however the term *classe* appears in this work only on a handful of occasions.

[2] *Wealth of Nations*, 1776.

[3] 'Three different orders of people . . . those who live by rent . . . those who live by wages . . . those who live by profit . . . Merchants and master manufacturers are, in this order, the two classes of people who commonly employ the largest capitals.' (*op. cit.*)

[4] See Chapter III.

[5] *Qu'est-ce que le tiers-état?*, 1789.

attack the remnants of estate privileges that persisted after the Restoration.[1]

Thus the term 'class' was used in an unspecified manner by Adam Smith, Madison and the other writers of the eighteenth century as one of the possible synonyms of 'group' or 'estate' available in colloquial speech. For the French post-revolutionary writers, however, the word came to be a technical term. As such, its use was to spread through modern theories of social structure, through party programmes and ideological manifestos. It was to become naturalized in almost all European languages, hardly changing its sound but only its inflexion. In my view, the fact that this term requires no translation has contributed much to its international success. Marxism and the international workers' movement have of course played a great part in this international success. But the wide use of the term 'class', in the sense of 'social class', in the contemporary United States and in European bourgeois milieux in the nineteenth century can undoubtedly be traced to a different and pre-Marxian origin.

In Poland, as elsewhere in the first half of the nineteenth century, the two terms 'class' and 'estate' were often used interchangeably. People referred to the 'middle estate' or the 'middle class', or spoke of seeking wives from the women who belong to their own estate or their own class. In his monumental dictionary of the Polish language (published between 1807 and 1814) Bogumil Linde defined a 'class in the society' in terms of 'estate' or 'sphere'. As examples he gave 'artisan, working, industrial, clerical; upper, middle, lower, lowest; wealthy, poor'. In most of these expressions nobody would at that time have objected to the substitution of the term 'estate', as in 'clerical estate', 'artisan estate' and so on. On the other hand, it would even at that early date have been difficult in some cases to substitute the term 'estate' for 'class', e.g. in such expressions as 'working class', or 'refined class'.

The writings of Joachim Lelewel[2] afford us some typical instances of the way in which 'estate' and 'class' were used in that

---

[1] On the other hand, both Saint-Simon and his followers used the term 'class' to denote narrower groups, as for instance when they speak of 'various working classes' and of 'the idle classes'. We find the same dual use of the term in other writers of the nineteenth century. For example, Marx and his school speak of the 'working class' and 'working classes', of the 'middle class' and the 'middle classes', of the 'propertied class' and the 'propertied classes,' etc.

[2] A Polish historian and a friend of Mazzini, Herzen and Marx.

period. In the same study both terms appear with frequency as synonymous to designate the most general concept of class.[1] Elsewhere 'class' is opposed to 'estate', the latter being interpreted in the same manner as in Diderot's *Encyclopaedia*.

Thus we find Lelewel making statements that sound quite contradictory. On some pages he speaks of the 'peasant estate', while on others he writes that 'the peasants did not constitute an estate, they were merely a distinct class'; they did not constitute an estate because they did not have any civic rights. Finally, Lelewel uses the term 'class' in the freest possible way to denote a group which is neither opposed to nor coincides with an estate.

During the nineteenth century, 'class' generally replaced the older term 'estate' in expressions which did not refer to legal criteria, particularly in expressions in which the term 'class' was used in its most general meaning: that is to say, when it referred to the basic groups in different societies. 'Class' ousted 'estate' in social theories, ideological declarations and the programmes of social movements. The only complication arose from the fact that as a consequence of socialist propaganda the word 'class' and its derivative expressions gradually came to be regarded as typical of certain milieux and acquired a 'class flavour'. For this reason, as Tawney once wrote, the use of these words in well-bred society was regarded as almost indecent.[2]

## Synonymity and Diversity of Meanings

The social changes which took place in the era in which the term 'class' became a part of the language of the social sciences

[1] 'Why is it that the Poles, who have for sixty years fought the oppressors of their country, cannot break their bonds? It may be that the walls erected and not yet broken down between the various classes of inhabitants, will prove to be the most essential cause of this failure'. (from *Trzy konstytucje polskie 1791, 1807, 1815 porównal i różnice ich rozważyl Joachim Lelewel w toku 1831*. (*The three Polish constitutions of 1791, 1807 and 1815 compared and their differences evaluated by Joachim Lelewel, 1831*, Poznan, 1861, pp. 7–8. 'The non-noble estate had no significance; the (urban) estate had another law than the noble estate, but the (rural) estate was subordinated to the noble estate.' (*ibid.*, p. 44) '. . . But although there is only one class that has a political right . . .' (*ibid.*, p. 8). 'Under Prussian and Austrian rule all the classees of the old (Polish) Republic were levelled down, all its estates, for the noble and the non-noble equally lost their rights completely, were equally deprived of political life, and became equally subjects under foreign rule and enslaved.' (*ibid.*, p. 100). (I am indebted to Mrs. H. W. for these quotations from Lelewel.)

[2] R. H. Tawney, *Equality*, London 1931, p. 66.

and social ideologies would seem to have exerted an interesting influence on the semantic functions of this term. I am thinking of a certain fundamental ambiguity of meanings which this term can have, an ambiguity which concerns the varying degree of generality of the term and which confuses the sense of certain general statements; the point here is the three-fold denotation of the term 'class', which is rather difficult to remove in the present terminology of the social sciences.

We have already noted that after the French Revolution the term 'class' ousted 'estate' with reference to the general concept of basic groups in a social structure. This happened in an era when the European societies were changing their social systems and when the old criteria which determined social divisions were giving place to new ones. In consequence, each of these terms, even when used in a general sense, came to represent a different period and to be associated with a different type of social structure.

In such conditions, the term 'class' acquired two meanings. In certain contexts the term was synonymous with 'estate', while in others it was differentiated, as in the statement that a class-structure had succeeded the estate-structure. When Adam Smith's followers spoke of three basic 'classes' where he used the term 'orders', or when Guizot expressed the view that there were no 'classes' left in France,[1] the term 'class' replaced the term 'order', which was previously used in similar circumstances (in Polish *stan*, in French *ordre* or *état*, in German *stand*). The new term came, however, to be specially associated with the social structure of bourgeois democracy, without losing its general meaning as the name of the basic groups in all societies, and this had certain consequences in the construction of general theories of social development and social structure.

The classic period of capitalism was, as we know, the period when economic power was at its peak. It was a period in which economic dependence dominated other forms of human relations to a degree never previously encountered. Money seemed to be able to buy all kinds of real privileges; the exploitation of labour was effected almost exclusively by means of the privilege of possessing the means of production, and the state was coming to be regarded, not by Marxists alone, as an executive committee of

[1] Cf. N. Assorodobraj: *Elements in the class consciousness of the bourgeoisie* (*Elementy świadomości klasowej mieszczaństwa* (Łódź, Przegląd Socjologiczny 1947.

the ruling class. The representatives of big business frequently did not trouble to conceal their belief that in 'civilized countries' persons who had large sums at their disposal could buy governments like so much merchandise.

Moreover, the people of this era expected further evolution in the same direction – particularly after the American Civil War and the ending of slavery in the United States, and before the establishment of a new customary caste-structure in the American way of life. The supposition that the next century could see the triumph of the principles on which the rule of Hitler was founded would have seemed to the people of that time incompatible with the laws of history. Their vision of the future approximated to an ideal type of society in which the power of capital would be the only form of authority and the relations of ownership the only determinant of the social-status system.

Like some of his forerunners, Marx and his followers associated the concept of class with the concept of the exploitation of other men's labour. But because in the days when capitalism flourished most abundantly the only form of mass exploitation of labour was exploitation based on the ownership of the means of production, the author of *Das Kapital* defined social classes in terms of their relation to the means of production (possession, non-possession, possession to a degree insufficient to permit the employment of hired labour). At the same time, this same term 'class' was used to describe the social structure of other 'formations', without troubling about the fact that 'class' was burdened with a meaning linked with a narrower range of phenomena.

In the latter part of his life Marx uttered a warning against the danger of applying generalizations reached after the investigation of the development of the capitalist societies of Western Europe to other periods in the history of mankind.[1] He himself did not however feel it necessary to differentiate between the two meanings of the term 'class', depending on whether he meant the classes characteristic of the structure of a capitalist society or the 'social classes' of every kind whose struggles were held to constitute the history of mankind from the disappearance of the original community of primitive society.

Because this differentiation of meaning is not made, the use of

[1] Letter to the Editor published in the Russian periodical, *Otcehestvennye Zapiski* (Fatherland Notes), November, 1877.

the Marxian or Leninist concept of class tends to suggest – contrary to certain assertions made by both Engels and Lenin – that all class divisions have been based simply on a difference in relations to the means of production, and that all class rule, all exploitation of other men's labour, has been achieved by a class monopoly of the ownership of the means of production.

Today it seems clear that when we study the problems of social structure as problems of systems of human inter-relationships, problems concerned with the privileges of power and wealth, problems of social inequalities and exploitation, we need a distinct general term. Such a term should cover not only social classes, in the narrower, non-institutional meaning characteristic of the structure of the bourgeois democracies, but also groups entering into the composition of systems in which the relation between possession of the means of production and control of the means of power takes a different form, as in the case of estate and caste systems. Here I have in mind a term of the kind which could also be applied in the analysis of post-capitalistic societies, where the division of the national income, the rise of privileged or underprivileged groups, and membership of these groups is to a considerable extent the result of deliberate decisions by the political authorities.

## A Superordinate Concept and a Two-fold Specification

In my account of the history of the relation between the terms 'class' and 'estate' I referred to the two-fold denotation of the term 'class'. This term is sometimes used in a general meaning in expressions where the term 'estate' would formerly have been used; at others it is used to characterize the social structure of modern capitalism, in contradistinction to the term 'estate' or to the term 'caste'. This contradistinction can in its turn be interpreted in two ways. In speaking of the contradistinction of terms we sometimes have in mind their correspondence to concepts which are mutually exclusive. In other cases we speak of terminological distinctions when the respective terms refer to concepts with a different content. In the first instance the extensions of the concepts are mutually exclusive, while in the second they may overlap. In the case of the term 'class' both interpretations are applicable.

In its narrower meaning, in which it is opposed to estates and castes, 'class' can be defined either by the negation of the attributes characterizing a caste or an estate or by criteria altogether inapplicable to what we have in mind when we speak of 'estates' or 'castes'. When, therefore, we have to do with the denotation of the term 'class' in application to problems of social structure, I see three possibilities, each of which has been and is made use of in sociological theories and in different accounts of the system of social relations, though not always with a distinct conceptual awareness.

1. In the general sense each group which is regarded as one of the basic components of the social structure may be called a 'class' of the social structure. I shall be considering the interpretation of the expression 'one of the basic components of the social structure' in the following chapter. In any case such a comprehensive concept includes both estate and caste, and also class in the second and third meanings distinguished here.

2. Of the two specifying versions of the concept of class which I should like to consider here, the first shows us a social class as a group distinguished in respect of the relations of property. We formulate this criterion in a quite general way, or rather we indicate only the kind of criterion involved, because this version, i.e. the economic version of the concept of social class, may vary in content in different definitions. This framework allows room for the definitions of both Adam Smith and Madison, for the age-old division of men into rich, poor and moderately well-to-do, for the Marxian division of classes according to their relation to the means of production, and for the economic definition of social class found in the early American sociologists (Ward, Small, Giddings and Cooley).

The economic criteria which are involved in the concept of class in all varieties of this version neither coincide with nor exclude the criteria which determine the extension of such concepts as estate or caste. Some caste or estate-systems can at the same time be economic-class systems, but such a coincidence can only be empirically established. In cases where such a coincidence does apply one can speak of the 'class' aspect of caste relations or the 'estate' aspect of the class-system.

In a somewhat different meaning it is also possible to speak of the 'class' aspect of an estate-system or a caste-system even when the coincidence does not occur, if we assume that between an estate-system and a class-system there holds some more or less complicated causal dependence. This is precisely the Marxian assumption. The view, not formulated by the Marxists, that all the historical struggles between estates, which are not separate classes in the economic sense, were in reality disguised class struggles, would correspond to the well-known view about the true nature of the religious conflicts in history.

3. In the second version specifying the concept of class, the class-system is contrasted with group-systems in the social structure in which an individual's membership of a group is institutionally determined and in which privileges or discriminations result from an individual's ascription to a certain group. In contradistinction to such groups of a caste or estate type, a class in this version is a group of which membership is not assigned by a birth-certificate nor any official document, such as a title of no-bility or an act of manumission, but is the consequence of social status otherwise achieved. The privileges and discriminations, which in this case require no sanction from any source, are not the effect but the cause of the individual's placement in the capitalist or proletarian class: one is reckoned among the capitalists because one possesses capital, and one belongs to the proletariat because one possesses no other sources of income than the capacity to hire out one's labour. The ideal type of privileges and discrimina-tions that fix an individual's social status regardless of the social categories to which this individual may belong are the economic privileges and discriminations found in a system of free competi-tion: property, income, the way in which one works for a living.

In various social systems one can observe two or more co-existing types of the relation of class dependence (using the term class in its widest sense). The two specifying versions of the con-cept of class are nevertheless most closely connected with an unrestricted capitalist system. In the former version, however, a class can at the same time be a caste or an estate, whereas in the latter these concepts are mutually exclusive. In contradistinction to groups whose composition and privileges have the sanction of political or religious institutions, a social class in the latter version comes into being 'spontaneously', by the force of events.

This is the usual way in which the term 'class' is used by con-temporary sociologists of a non-Marxist persuasion. Hence we find the terms 'caste' and 'class' contrasted in dictionaries of the social sciences, and hence such titles as 'Caste and Class in a Southern Town'.

Incidentally we should note that, as seen from the viewpoint of the third conception, social classes, in the sense of so-called 'high society' and in general classes in a scheme of synthetic gradation,[1] should be regarded as a sort of synthesis of caste and class – at least in societies where some estate traditions survive.

Because of the absence of terminological distinctions, 'class' has different meanings in different contexts. It means one thing when one speaks of the 'overlapping of a caste and a class structure', and something else when we speak of the 'history of class societies' or the 'history of the class struggle'. In these cases the meaning of the term is determined by its context. This may not evoke misunderstandings as to the denotation of the term, but it does imply the risk mentioned above. Moreover the burdening of the term 'class' with an ambiguous content makes it more difficult to analyse the structure of modern societies with nationalised means of production.

## Terminological Suggestions

The adjustment of the terminology to the conceptual apparatus can be affected in two ways. If we keep the term 'class' for the superordinate concept, we shall have to use specifying qualifications for 'class' in its second and third meanings. Thus the 'overlapping of an estate and a class structure', used with reference to Poland in the great period of the *szlachta*, or to France under the last Bourbons, would be an overlapping of two different social-class systems, like the 'overlapping of a caste and a class structure' in the United States or India.

On the other hand, if, following prevailing usage in modern sociology, the term 'class' is reserved for the narrower concept in its first or second version, it will be necessary to find a term for the more comprehensive concept. This is no easy task if we wish to avoid introducing semantic conventions which completely disregard the usage of colloquial speech and the terminological traditions of the social sciences.

[1] Cf. p. 44.

# Chapter IX

## THE CONCEPT OF SOCIAL CLASS: A COMMON MODEL AND DISCREPANT DEFINITIONS

### In Search of a Common Conceptual Content

IN GENERAL conceptions of social structure, especially where different forms of social order are involved, we usually have to deal with the widest concept of class, just as we do in general theories concerned with the class determination of cultural phenomena. But even when matters are not complicated by the threefold denotation of the term 'social class' discussed in the foregoing chapter, this has been interpreted in various ways, not only in colloquial speech but also in scientific literature, as the divergent definitions of class bring out clearly.

We now have to consider whether the conceptions which we are comparing have any common ground, and to what extent the representatives of different viewpoints are in agreement about the basic characteristics of social structure in respect of which they speak of the 'class' character of societies. To put this differently, we are faced by the question: what common conceptual content can be found in definitions which disagree with each other?

It seems to me that we can point to at least three generally accepted assumptions relating to the concept of class and the 'class' society. These appear most frequently in the form of implicit assumptions discoverable in the course of discussion. The main reasons why these assumptions are usually not explicitly formulated in definitions is that they seem to be self-explanatory or that they are implied by the definition. If they seem self-explanatory, it is because they are generally accepted.

The three assumptions which appear to be common to all conceptions of a 'class' society can be stated in the following manner:

1. The classes constitute a system of the most comprehensive groups in the social structure.

2. The class division concerns social statuses connected with a system of privileges and discriminations not determined by biological criteria.

3. The membership of individuals in a social class is relatively permanent.

In the first assumption two elements must be distinguished: (*a*) that classes are the most comprehensive groups; (*b*) that classes form a system of such groups. By the most comprehensive groups in the social structure I understand here a small number of groups – two or more – differentiated in consequence of the division of society according to criteria that are important in social life. The second element introduced by this assumption involves treating a class as a member of a certain system of relations. This means that the definition of any class must take into account the relation of this class to the other groups in this system. To explain who is a proletarian in the Marxian sense we must bring in the concept of a capitalist. When we speak of a middle class we assume the existence of a lower class and an upper class. This constitutes a fundamental distinction between a social class and occupational groups, irrespective of their size. In this respect occupational groups can be compared with ethnic or religious groups; they can be described without reference to their relation with each other. Thus at the moment when we begin to regard an occupational group for example, farmers, priests, or warriors in certain social systems, as a component of the system of basic groups in a social structure, this occupational group become a social class, without ceasing – from another viewpoint – to be an occupational group. In the same way, an ethnic or religious group can also in certain cases become a social class.

The second assumption has been formulated in so general a manner as to be applicable both to divisions made with reference to the functions of the different classes in economic life and to divisions concerned with the relative share in the national income. It has also been formulated in such a way that class divisions may include divisions corresponding to a system of non-economic privileges and discriminations (some caste-systems) or to a system of privileges and discriminations dependent in different ways on economic status but not directly fixed by it. We have encountered such divisions in, for instance, conceptions of synthetic gradation. The assumption under discussion refers equally to groups differentiated, as it were, by an absolute division of privileges and discriminations (privileged and under-privileged groups) and to groups which differ from one another *in the type* of privileges and discriminations associated with them. In this way, this assumption can be applied even when it is accepted that each class has its privileges and its duties, associated with different social functions, as some supporters of the class system have tried to show with the aid of a functional interpretation of inter-class relations. The reservation with regard to biological criteria excludes the privileges and discriminations assigned directly by sexual criteria.

In the third assumption I am thinking of the sort of situation in which a transition from one group to another is made by some individuals only, and where the rule is rather to remain within one's own group throughout one's life. Herein social classes differ from levels in an official hierarchy or from the age-groups that play so important a part in the structure of pre-capitalist societies, and particularly in the so-called 'primitive' societies. The relative permanence of class membership constitutes a necessary condition of a 'class' society according, it would seem, to all the conceptions which we have considered.

## Various Criteria and Common Assumptions

The three common assumptions just considered are, as I have already pointed out, usually accorded tacit acceptance. On the other hand, it is other characteristics of the social-class structure that are usually mentioned as the fundamental characteristics of a class-system. On the basis of the former implicit assumptions, we can discern in the latter characteristics different criteria of social classes. In the light of the discussion so far, it would seem that out of the whole variety of ways of conceiving the social structure, out of all the differing manners of understanding class, one can elicit three or four such characteristics. They are by no means of equal importance in the history of social thought.

1. The first of these characteristics is the vertical order of social classes: the existence of superior and inferior categories of social statuses, which are superior and inferior in respect of some system of privileges and discriminations. When one accepts such a criterion, 'class structure' means as much as 'class stratification'.

For a broader interpretation privileges and discriminations of all kinds can be involved, provided that they are socially significant. In a narrower interpretation we are concerned only with relations of wealth and power. Materially speaking, it is not very important which of these interpretations is chosen, because socially-significant privileges are usually included in the relations of wealth and power. The emphasis laid on the privileges of wealth and power seems to me advisable because of the connexion of the concept of class with the problems from which it arose, namely, the connexion with important practical problems and with the clashes between ideologies which make use of the term. For it is this connexion that gives the concept of class a particular importance. The Marxist theory of classes uses a still narrower criterion, taking as the basis of the vertical order the privilege of exploiting other men's labour. The classes are placed in a hierarchical order with reference to this fundamental privilege, which is conditioned by the different relations of particular classes to the means of production.

2. The second characteristic is the distinctness of permanent class interests (a 'class' society being regarded as a society that is divided into large groups with distinct, important and permanent interests). In a more extreme interpretation, one would speak not of the distinctness of class interests but of their conflicts: according to the traditional Smithian view, developed and popularized by the founders of Marxism, the source of these conflicts is to be found in the different modes of sharing in the national income, which are conditioned by different relations to the means of production.[1]

---

[1] We speak of the *distinctness* of class interests when what serves or does not serve the interest of one class does not affect the interest of another class. The *conflict* of interests arises when something that serves the interest of one class is to the disadvantage of another class and *vice versa*. One can obviously speak of conflicts of class interests both from the viewpoint of the classes concerned and from the viewpoint of the theorist, who may consider that the members of this or that class are not generally aware of their 'essential' class interests.

3. The third characteristic is class consciousness. The content of this concept may be more or less comprehensive. It may involve not only class identification but also a consciousness of the place of one's class in the class-hierarchy, a realization of class distinctness and class interests and, possibly, of class solidarity as well. A 'class' society in this sense is a society in which the majority of active members possess class consciousness, and this is reflected in their behaviour.

4. Finally, the fourth of those characteristics which can provide a basis for belief that a given society is a 'class' society is social isolation. The absence of closer social contacts; social distance – this is the behavioural criterion of class divisions, which undoubtedly plays an important part in the social consciousness of different milieux, and not only in caste and estate cultures. On this criterion is based the definition of class used by some social scientists in the United States: according to this definition a social class is the largest group of people whose members have intimate social access to one another.[1] Using this sort of criterion, some observers in the last quarter of the nineteenth century divided Warsaw society into five social classes. A society is a 'class' society in respect of this characteristic if there exist within it distinct barriers to social intercourse and if class boundaries can be drawn by means of an analysis of inter-personal relations.

When one speaks of the 'class' character of a given society from this viewpoint, one usually finds that not only is social isolation involved but also the effects of this isolation and the effects of differences in the degree of access to the means of consumption. Here I am thinking of cultural cleavages and the feeling that people belonging to different classes are strangers to each other. The members of different classes differ in customs and modes of behaviour and speech. The latter may be differences of vocabulary and pronunciation, or differences in the actual language spoken. In Haiti, the members of the upper class speak French, while lower

[1] A. Davis and J. Dollard, *Children of Bondage*, Washington, p. 13. See also *ibid.*, p. 259. (Both quotations are taken from Myrdal, *op. cit.*, pp. 673, 1378.) J. Schumpeter accepts as a criterion of class in racially homogeneous milieux a connexion expressed by the range of marital eligibility. 'We find a suitable definition of the class – one that makes it outwardly recognisable and involves no class theory (*sic.*) – in the fact that intermarriage prevails among its members, socially rather than legally.' 'Imperialism and Social Theory', 1951, quoted from *Class, Status and Power*, ed. Bendix and Lipset, Routledge and the Free Press, 1953, p. 77.

class people speak Creole.[1] The feeling of class distance with which
the educated strata regarded the 'mob' was brought out in an
arresting manner by the Polish writer Stefan Żeromski in his
*Homeless People*, written in 1898. In 1936, L. W. Doob describing
the 'poor whites' in the Southern States, wrote that the people of
this class could be distinguished even in their appearance from
other inhabitants of Southern towns as easily as a Negro could be
distinguished by his pigmentation.[2] In the period preceding the
changes of recent years in post-war Poland, the witty Warsaw
cockneys defined the two classes in socialist countries by the
terms 'proletariat' and 'chevroletariat'.[3]

Disraeli compared the two social classes in England to two

[1] The Haitian *langue créole* is a peculiar mixture of French dialect and Spanish,
with a few African elements. A recent book by B. Ryan affords an eloquent example
of the fourth criterion of the class character of a society in post-war Ceylon. Here
the two basic urban classes are 'an English-educated, shoe-and-trousers-wearing,
white-collar and professional upper class, and the saronged, barefooted vernacular-
speaking labor class'. *Caste in Modern Ceylon*, New Brunswick, 1953; quotation from
the review of this study in the *American Sociological Review*, Oct. 1954.

[2] L. W. Doob: 'Poor Whites: a Frustrated Class' (published as an appendix to
John Dollard's book: *Caste and Class in a Southern Town*, New York, 1949, first published 1937.)

In an article already cited, M. Rosenberg writes: 'An important social characteristic likely to engender awareness of class differences are styles of life visibly represented by consumption items. In large parts of Europe the rich are clearly set off
from the poor by items requiring a large financial investment, such as bath tubs and
inside plumbing, the possession of automobiles, the wearing of a suit for weekday
use. In mediaeval Europe the classes (or estates) could be visibly differentiated by
the possession of horses and armor.' 'Perceptual Obstacles to Class Consciousness',
*Social Force*, Oct. 1953.

[3] Before 1956 there was a raising of wage-scales in various sectors in Poland, in
which the benefit went for the most part to those who had previously earned most.
I heard this wage-policy defended on the following economic grounds. The small
stocks of consumer goods available in the country – so ran the argument – make it
impossible to raise the wages of the majority of employees. On the other hand, an
increase in the income of those whose earnings are several times higher than the
average does not constitute a threat to the stock of consumer goods which the mass
of people are interested in obtaining. This is so not only because only relatively
small numbers of people are affected but above all because the budget of those who
earn high wages contains different items. An increase in their incomes will not produce an increase in the consumption of bread, butter, sausage or cheap clothing, nor
will it swell the crowds in cheap eating-houses; instead it will be used for luxuries
which could not in any case have figured in the budget of people who earn less than
the average. In this connexion it was explained that the importation or production of
luxury goods is essential, either because of trade agreements, or of the need to develop production techniques, or for prestige reasons. So far as I know, these arguments had a real influence on the decisions taken by the makers of economic policy
in Poland, and probably in other countries with a socialist economy as well. If the
premises on which the arguments are based correspond to reality, it means that in a

nations,[1] and the same comparison may be encountered in Engels' study of the conditions of the English working class published in 1845. Contemporary Soviet writers regard a distinctive 'socio-political and spiritual profile'[2] as one of the fundamental class characteristics, in a similar way as those American sociologists who regard class as a socio-psychological phenomenon.[3]

## The Interdependence of Characteristics

The class criteria enumerated above are not independent of one another. It is hard to doubt that social stratification – a class hierarchy of privileges and discriminations – implies conflicts of class interests. Class consciousness and class isolation find their explanation in class stratification and conflict of interests. Those who take class consciousness as a criterion of the class-system, as contemporary American sociologists do, do not question the 'objectivity' of the conditions from which this consciousness arises.

If the characteristics which we have specified as different versions of the criterion of a class-system are inter-dependent, then various definitions of a class society may in reality differ less between themselves than one would believe in view of the different formulations. Although one or another characteristic may be used in particular definitions of a class society, the description of that society which supplements the definitions may contain all these characteristics. At this point the differences between the different conceptions may be reduced above all to differences of opinion as to which trait of a 'class society' is regarded as 'primary', the most important from the viewpoint of causal dependence, or the most distinctive or the most socially-significant in some other respects.

[1] *Sybil or the Two Nations,* London, 1845.

[2] T. Gubariev, 'O priodolenii klassovykh razlichii v SSSR' (About the overcoming of class differences in the U.S.S.R.), *Bolshevik,* 1951, No. 5.

[3] Those in this country who speak of the 'middle class' as our largest cohesive social group. . . . refer to those millions of Americans who share, in general, common values, attitudes and aspirations. Such spokesmen reiterate a view presented 'scientifically' by the Sociological Fathers'. Charles H. Page, *Class and American Sociology,* New York, 1940, p. 254.

socialist country too we could be faced with some traits of a social structure consisting of two collectivities, each living in an entirely different manner – according to the indices of consumption, as envisaged by our fourth criterion of a class system. The terms 'proletariat' and 'chevroletariat' used above are a way of expressing the sociological aspect of an economic harmony of this kind.

Do we follow Marx in placing the main emphasis on the system of privileges and discriminations, on exploitation and in general on asymmetrical relations of dependence? Or do we follow Madison or Max Weber (when he is speaking of class structure) in stressing the distinctness of interests? Or again, are we at one with modern American sociologists in acknowledging class consciousness as the most socially-important fact in the domain of inter-group relations, and do we, in describing a 'class' society – despite the suggestive terminology – give primacy to the characteristics which Weber links with his concept of an estate, not with the concept of class?[1]

Differences of opinion as to the essence of the 'class' nature of 'class' societies are not however only a matter of emphasis. If the different criteria which are taken as the basis of various definitions of a 'class' society are not independent of one another, this does not mean that one can assume that they are permanently present together. The various conceptions may differ not only in respect of the particular characteristic of the class-system which they single out as fundamental but also because some take three or four conditions into consideration, while others take only two. The common basic assumptions concerned with the concept of class sometimes make it difficult to see clearly whether, when faced by discrepant definitions, we are in fact dealing with differences of conceptual apparatus or with contradictory views regarding the scope of the phenomena which is established by these common assumptions.

### 'Class' Character as a Characteristic of Social Structure Admitting of Gradation

A society may be more or less class-divided and its 'class' character may be more or less rich in content. In Chapter V, I pointed out that Marx, in calling a class without class consciousness

---

[1] 'In contrast to classes, status groups (*Stände*) are normally communities. They are however, often of a rather amorphous kind. In contrast to the purely economically determined 'class situation', we wish to designate as 'status situation' every typical component of the life fate of men that is determined by a specific, positive or negative, social estimation of *honor*. This honor may be connected with any quality shared by a plurality. . . . In content, status honor is normally expressed by the fact that above all else a specific style of life can be expected from all those who wish to belong to the circle.' (From Max Weber, *Essays in Sociology*, Routledge & Kegan Paul, 1947, pp. 186–7.)

a 'stratum' or a 'class in itself' (*Klasse an sich*), in contrast to a 'class for itself' (*Klasse für sich*), was expressing his conviction that a class fully deserves the name of 'class' only if its members are conscious of class interests and feel class solidarity. Without accepting any one particular characteristic as a necessary condition of a class-system, one can nevertheless regard such a characteristic as an important factor in intensifying the 'class' nature of a society.

Moreover, probably all the characteristics with which we are concerned here admit of gradation. This is true of the permanence of class membership, that is to say of the stability of class divisions. In other words, in different 'class' societies there exists a differing degree of probability that an individual will remain in his class until the end of his life. An extreme example of this is caste-affiliation, which is life-long, determined before the individual's birth and passed on unconditionally to his descendants. At the other extreme would be the society that satisfies the ideals of Lincoln, who approved of all the three social statuses that correspond to Marx's three basic classes, provided that each man should be able during his lifetime to achieve each of the three statuses, beginning as a hired labourer, later working for himself, and with the hope that in the future he himself might be able to benefit from the hired labour of others.[1]

Other characteristics admitting of gradation are those concerned with the distinctness of class boundaries, the range of social inequalities, and the cleavages or conflicts of class interests. Class consciousness is also a matter of degree, both where it concerns the prevalence of class consciousness and also its content and emotional charge. Finally, 'class' societies differ in the degree of social isolation and social contacts across class boundaries. There is a wide range in this respect between the *mores* of contemporary Scandinavian countries and those found in societies with estate traditions, like Spain, Hungary, or Poland in the second half of the nineteenth century. Nor should we forget caste-societies, where group separation is supported by severe formal sanctions.

In addition, a society may be regarded as more or less class-divided both with regard to the *number* of class criteria which it

[1] 'I want every man to have a chance – and I believe a black man is entitled to it – in which he can better his condition – when he may look forward and hope to be a hired laborer this year and next, work for himself afterwards, and finally to hire men to work for him. That is the true system.' Speech in New Haven, 6 March 1860, quoted by Myrdal, *op. cit.*, p. 670.

displays and the *degree* to which particular class characteristics can be attributed to it. From this viewpoint we can compare different societies as historical phenomena, and also different images of the same society.

## The Model of a Class as a Basic Group

Like other concepts relating to social life and culture the concept of class has been formed according to a model adopted by way of exemplification. If my earlier examination is accurate in this respect, the same model corresponds closely to different conceptions of class, even when these give discrepant definitions.

The model of a class is made up of several different characteristics admitting of gradation. Several criteria overlap in it, and the absence of one criterion may be offset by a higher degree of another characteristic, just as in the evaluation of a work of art a lower level of artistic technique may be offset, for instance, by originality of idea or power of expression. A work of art can be a work of art to a greater or lesser degree, just as a social class may be a class to a greater or lesser degree.

The point now is to determine the limit: what deviations from the model are permissible? The criteria which make up the model of a social class are not commensurable, any more than the criteria which make up the model of a work of art. There is no objective measure which would enable one to establish the degree of originality in a work of art which would make up for a certain degree of technical deficiency. Nor is there an objective measure which could establish the degree of rigidity of class boundaries which could offset, say, a lack of class consciousness. As the criteria are not commensurable, the final decision as to what is and what is not a social class must ultimately be reached by intuitive judgments made in a given milieu about the importance of various criteria (compare the conceptions of American sociologists), or by considering practical consequences and the requirements of action (compare the Marxist theory of class).

## Exhaustive and Non-Exhaustive Divisions

The extension of the concept of class becomes narrower or wider according to the degree of strictness with which one regards deviations from the model of the particular class concept used, according to the degree of tolerance employed in offsetting one criterion against another. If the concept of class is strictly applied, it may not cover all the groups that are differentiated in the social structure. In that event not every member of the society will belong to a class, just as in the Indian caste system there are people who do not belong to any caste.

The division of a society into classes may therefore be either an exhaustive or a non-exhaustive one, for, depending on the way in which class is conceived, a society may be either a system of classes, or a system of classes and groups that resemble classes to a certain degree but are not comprised in the concept of class. As I have already said, the Marxist usually call these groups 'strata'; thus a society may, according to the Marxist conception, be composed not only of classes but also of 'strata' which do not fall under any class. In this respect, Marx in his '18th Brumaire' took up an indecisive position in respect of the French peasantry, an important component of French society which deviated from the class model in its lack of consciousness of class interests.

According to Marx and the Marxists, the *lumpenproletariat* is not a class because it does not take part in the process of production. Nor, though for quite other reasons, is the intelligentsia a class. In this case the deviation from the model is excessive. On the other hand, Stalin and his followers considered that the deviation of the 'non-antagonistic classes' in the Soviet Union from the model of class, a model which after all included class antagonism as one of its characteristics, did not prevent the working class and the *kolchoz* – peasantry – in the Soviet Union from being recognised as classes. In this Stalinist conception of society, in which there are classes without class antagonisms and without class stratification, only the intelligentsia would not fall under the concept of class and would be named a 'stratum'.

American and West European sociologists, for whom the term 'social class' does not fulfil those social functions which it was made to perform by the Marxian school of thought, have conceived the concept of class so widely that the division into classes may be an exhaustive division, that is to say, that every individual in the society may be included in a social class. Only if they conceive social structure from a different point of view do they make use of the term 'stratum'. Although it differs from the division of society into classes, the division of society into strata is also an exhaustive one.

## Types of Deviation from the Model

The deviations from the model are not only a question of defining the concept of class with a broader or narrower scope. The various conceptions which start from the same model differ not only in the degree of permissible deviations or in the exhaustive or non-exhaustive nature of the division of society into classes but also in the type of deviation. In the different conceptions the emphasis is laid on one or another of the various characteristics contained in the model of social class; one or another characteristic is regarded as the 'basic' one, and the extension of the concept of class permits one or another form of compensation, both as regards the choice of characteristics chosen for such compensation and the differing degree in which these characteristics should be present. Differences of this kind occur not only when we are dealing with different schemes of social structure but also when we are concerned with the same scheme applied to different cases. We noted this in the instance of the dichotomic scheme as interpreted by the followers of Saint-Simon and, on the other hand, by Babeuf or the authors of the *Communist Manifesto*.

## The Model of a Proletarian and the Denotation of the Proletariat

Indistinct images of class structure may not only have their origin in deviations from the model of a social class; they may also stem from the models of particular classes. In the Marxist view of social classes in a capitalistic system the social class *par excellence*, the class which is nearest to the general model of a class, is the proletariat, and the Marxist model of a proletarian is that of a class-conscious factory worker. The Marxist model of the proletariat does not coincide in extension with the Marxist definition, which gives as characteristics defining the proletarian the fact of working for hire and a low share in the national income (a share that does not correspond to the 'surplus value' produced by the proletarian).

The definition allows manifold deviations from the model of a proletarian, for it also covers wage-workers who are not

CONCEPTUAL CONSTRUCTS AND SOCIAL REALITY

class-conscious, those who do not work in factories and those who do not do manual work. When the boundaries of the proletariat are being drawn, the first two of these 'deviant' groups do not give rise to any doubts. Marxism recognises both proletarians who lack class-consciousness and an agricultural or cottage-industry proletariat. On the other hand, the Marxist standpoint with regard to the third category, that of hired workers who do not work with their hands, is uncertain. The founders of Marxism and their followers often use the terms 'proletariat' and 'working class' as synonyms. If manual labour is not included in the set of criteria that define a proletarian then the proletariat is not co-extensive in scope with the working class; but if manual labour is included, then white-collar workers, who have a low share in the national income, do not belong to any class.

## Conceptual Precision and Practical Requirements

In sociological studies attempts to provide a precise concept of class have been expressed in a number of definitions which suggest a new usage of the term (henceforth to be called 'projecting definitions') and in suggestions proposing certain terminological distinctions.

But the concept of class has long been an *idée force* in social movements and the term 'class' has become an instrument of action. In changing circumstances an instrument is more convenient when it lends itself to many uses. For a politician or for a social leader a discussion of the extension of the concept of class is academic. In general discussions he works with models: the proletariat *par excellence* is more convenient on such occasions than the proletariat determined according to one definition or another. In the same way it is more convenient in general discussions to use the concept of class *par excellence*. When one turns to concrete problems, on the other hand, the extension of the concepts is widened according to need and greatly exceeds that of the model. At the same time a suggestion is left that the designata of both terms correspond to the models originally used.

# Chapter X

## TYPES OF INTERPRETATION OF THE SOCIAL STRUCTURE – AN ATTEMPT AT CLASSIFICATION

### Ordering Relations and Relations of Dependence in Class-Systems

WITH THE assumption that a class is a component of a system of basic groups as our starting-point, we shall be able to sum up the conclusions reached in earlier chapters more lucidly, to bring out certain problems that have so far been overlooked and to give a more distinct outline of a typology of schemes of social structure, a typology which has emerged from our earlier analyses.

The relations of which we can make use when we speak of a class-system are, as we have seen, of a two-fold nature: ordering relations and relations of dependence. This distinction emerged in the opening chapter, when I was discussing the concept of structure in its most general meaning.

Two basic interpretations of social class correspond to these two kinds of relations. We have to do with the first interpretation when the class division is conceived of as a division into groups differentiated according to the degree in which they possess the characteristic which constitutes the criterion of division, as, for instance, income-level. Since these groups are arranged in a system of superior and inferior classes according to the degree in which they display the particular characteristic, class structure carries or has the same meaning here as class stratification. As T. H. Marshall pointed out in his study of class conflict:

'We are discussing a particular kind of group whose nature is indicated by the phrase "social stratification". The groups, that is to say, lie one above the other in layers.'[1]

In the second interpretation social classes form a system according to their one-sided or mutual dependence, dependence being understood in both cases as a dependence based on causal relationships.

We came across the first way of understanding the class system in our analysis of American conceptions in Chapters III and VII. The second emerged in the schemes of social structure which were discussed in Chapters II, IV, and V. The same system of social classes is often regarded simultaneously as a system based on relations of dependence and as a system of gradation.[2]

Early in the first chapter I drew the reader's attention to the wider connexions between the two kinds of relations. Later, these questions re-emerged during my analysis of the Marxian conception, in connexion with the coincidence between class functions and degree of wealth. Although the categories of capitalist, petit bourgeois and proletarian are differentiated on the basis of their differing relations to the means of production, they can at the same time be ranked on a general scale according to income-level. Statistically, there is a correlation between income and the type of relation to the means of production. This correlation is brought out in the Marxian theory of classes in a manner beyond any doubt.

The relation of superiority and inferiority between classes differentiated according to functional criteria can of course be based on something other than the degree of wealth. One instance of this is found in the Hindu caste gradations; another might be in the supremacy of the 'working class' amongst the 'non-antagonistic classes' of the Soviet conception, where classes are distinguished according to the type of ownership of the means of production and the source of income.[3]

[1] 'The Nature of Class Conflict' in *Class Conflict and Social Stratification* (ed. T. H. Marshall), Le Play House, London, 1938.
[2] 'Les classes, ce sont les fonctions. La grosse difficulté est celle-ci: d'ou vient la hierarchie des fonctions?' *Grande Encyclopèdie*, Paris, Vol XI, *Classes Sociales*, p. 570.
[3] T. Gubariev, 'O priodolenii klassovykh razlichii v SSSR' (About the overcoming of class differences in the U.S.S.R.), *Bolshevik*, 1951, No. 5.

In all such cases we can regard the system of dependence and the system of gradation not only as two different aspects of the same reality but as two different aspects of the same division of the same reality.

### Two Interpretations of Mutual Dependence

In describing the second way of understanding class-systems, I spoke of relations of one-sided or mutual dependence. An asymmetric relation of dependence in social relationships is usually conceived as a relation of subjection to another's power. In conceptions of class structure mutual dependence may have two meanings. The first is that of an 'organic' dependence. Groups are mutually necessary to one another since each performs different functions. The second meaning refers to a negative correlation of interests – the advances of one class are the set-backs of the other.

We encountered the first meaning in the class-system of Adam Smith, in the views of the physiocrats which were criticised by Mably, and in Spencer's conception of the social organism. One may also recall at this point the medieval interpretation of society as consisting of three estates which are essential to one another: those who pray, those who defend the country and those who work. We have come across the second meaning in all cases where the conception of class involves class antagonism: e.g. in Madison, Babeuf, Marx and his disciples, and also in some contemporary writers who are far removed from Marxism, like Sorokin. The view of classes as essentially antagonistic groups is also found in Touraine's report of 1953.[1]

### Criteria of Internal Cohesion

The distinction between two basic types of understanding class systems is not dependent on the type of criterion taken as determining class affiliations, such as class consciousness or purely 'objective' criteria. Nor does it depend on whether cultural criteria or the criterion of social intercourse between classes are applied in determining class boundaries.

[1] 'Rapport sur la préparation en France de l'enquête internationale sur la stratification et la mobilité sociale.' Cf. pp. 53–54.

We noted that some sociologists use the criterion of social inter-course between classes in their definitions of social class. For Davis and Dollard a social class is the largest group of people between whom intimate social contact can exist, whereas relations between the classes are characterized by an absence of 'intimate participation' between members of different classes. For Schumpter the boundaries of a social class are coextensive with the range within which socially permissible marriages may be contracted. These writers regard classes as groupings whose members are linked to one another by virtue of an internal social bond, and inter-class relations as relations characterized by strangeness, social distance or antagonism.

If we accept the assumption that classes are groups which con-stitute a system of groups in a social structure, we must remember that 'social bond', *esprit de corps*, 'social intercourse', 'absence of intimate participation' are insufficient criteria to permit one to recognize a class-system in the groups thus differentiated. A system – understood as an arrangement in which each component has its position fixed by its relations to other components – can be constructed only by means of ordering relations or relations of dependence.

On the other hand, *esprit de corps*, social consciousness, social intercourse, and 'class' culture are characteristics whose coinci-dence with class boundaries in a system established in another manner is very important in the 'class' character of a society. I dis-cussed this in Chapter IX, where I considered in what respects the 'class' character of a society might admit of gradation. Amongst other concepts this involved the Marxian distinction between a 'class in itself', and a 'class for itself'.

In systems based on ordering relations, that is to say systems of gradations of social classes, the characteristics that determine the internal cohesion of social groups are usually treated as a criterion in determining inter-class boundaries: for instance, be-tween the lower, middle and upper classes or between the lower, middle, upper-middle and upper classes (cf. Chapter III). As we noted, all the American sociologists who consider classes in American society as something more than statistical categories have referred to the phenomenon of social consciousness and have often treated the range of social contacts or cultural dif-ferences as a verifying test of whether the division into classes in a system of gradation is not merely a conventional division, or whether it has a genuine foundation in social reality.[1]

## Class Attributes and Types of Dependence in the Dichotomic and the Functional Schemes

In earlier chapters we considered three basic schemes of class structure and also the conception of a classless, non-egalitarian society. Two of these schemes, the dichotomic and the functional, present the social structure as a system of dependence, the third as a system of gradation. In schemes based on relations of dependence the various terms in the system are characterized by different attributes; in a scheme of gradation they are characterized by a differing degree of the same characteristic.[2]

We distinguish the dichotomic scheme not because it consists of two components but because we describe the components of this system in terms of opposite attributes: working class and non-working class; exploiters and exploited; rulers and ruled; propertied and non-propertied classes. This means that classes in a dichotomic scheme are terms of an asymmetric relation, this relation being described as a one-sided dependence, involving authority or an overwhelming influence over the destinies of others. The slave lives under the rule of his master and the peasant under the rule of his landlord, while at a time of unemployment the worker is at the mercy of the capitalist. This does not however exclude a mutual functional dependence between the components involved in this asymmetric relation.

This sort of mutual dependence is brought about above all by antagonism: conflict of interests is of course a symmetrical relation.[3] But mutual dependence between classes with opposite attributes is sometimes regarded in a different way: as a dependence based on co-operation and the division of functions. It may be recalled that both in Aristotle and in Theodoret we encountered the view that the servants need the masters as much as the

[1] Cf. p. 122, note [2].
[2] Cf. Llewellyn Gross.
*An attribute* refers to a quality which has an all-or-none existence. A *variable* refers to a quality which exists in varying degrees.' 'The Use of the Class Concept in Social Research', *A.J.S.* March, 1949.
[3] The co-presence of a one-sided and a mutual dependence between the worker and the industrialist is brought out by, *inter alia*, Adam Smith.

masters need the servants. In arguments of this kind, we have to do with an attempt to assimilate the dichotomy of opposed classes to the scheme of mutual dependence, which we have called a functional scheme and which usually has three or more components.

The belief that the dependence of the exploited on the exploiters is a one-sided one has also been undermined in a different way and with a different purpose: that is to say, in the interest not of the ruling class but of the oppressed class. In his parable about the two cities, St. John Chrysostom strove to persuade his readers that the fortunes of the rich depend on the working class to a far greater extent than the fortunes of those who work depend on the rich. Shelley also stressed the same dependence in a more poetic vein,[1] and it is on this assumption that contemporary advocates of the general strike base their arguments. But the symmetrical relations which we come across in functional schemes are not involved in these cases. Nobody doubts that where there is a stable social order the dependence of the manufacturer on the worker is only a potential one. Those who, like Shelley, try to make the worker conscious of this potential dependence do so with the object of arousing him to liberate himself from the existing one-sided dependence, which runs in quite the opposite direction.

The terms in which the dichotomic scheme is usually formulated (rulers and ruled, exploiters and exploited, and so on) presume a one-sided dependence. Thus we regard the name 'dichotomic scheme' as an abbreviation of the expression 'dichotomic scheme of one-sided dependence' or 'dichotomic scheme with opposite attributes'.

Class attributes in a multiple functional scheme suggest mutual dependence, and are particularly suitable for emphasizing dependence based on collaboration and the division of functions. Those who live by rent, those who live by profit and those who live by wages in Adam Smith's scheme are mutually essential to one another.

But this division into three classes in terms of functions in the process of production is simultaneously a division in terms of the source of income (rents, profits, wages), while differences in the source of income combined with reciprocal dependencies lead to conflict of interests. Thus we find mutual dependence in both

[1] Song of the Men of England (see p. 26).

its aspects in Adam Smith's functional scheme. The second aspect – dependence through antagonism – emerges still more strongly in Madison. With Pareto too a negative correlation of interests applies not only between workers and capitalists but also between the two classes of capitalists which he distinguishes as *rentiers* and *entrepreneurs*, who co-operate with each other.[1]

Thus the two aspects of mutual dependence can be involved in conceptions both of dichotomic and multiple class-systems conceived of as a system of dependence, although a dichotomic scheme with opposite attributes is particularly suitable for emphasizing dependence based on co-operation.

## Two Interpretations of Dichotomy in the Marxian Scheme

In considering the classic Marxian scheme in Chapter V, I treated it as the result of the intersection of three dichotomies. In view, however, of the prospects of social development outlined by Marx, one should perhaps see in his conception of class structure rather one single dichotomy based on three criteria of division. In this interpretation the two basic classes are opposed to each other in respect of three pairs of opposite attributes. The class of people who possess the means of production, employ hired labour and do not work themselves[2] is contrasted with the class of those who do not possess the means of production, do not employ hired labour, but themselves work as hired labour.

This ideal type of dichotomic structure of a capitalist society has never had any real existence in the world about which Marx and his followers have written because the attributes have never been fully satisfied. The correspondence of these attributes with reality increases with increasing economic polarization of the society and decreases when the number of moderately prosperous individuals grows larger. But between the two classes which fulfil all three conditions of the ideal dichotomy there is the group of those who fail to fulfil one or two of the conditions for inclusion in one of the two classes. This is the sphere of the 'intermediate

---

[1] 'En réalité, ces deux catégories des "capitalistes" ont des intérêts souvent différents parfois opposés. Ils s'opposent même plus que ceux des classes dites des "capitalistes" et des "prolétaires"'. (*Traité de sociologie générale*, Paris 1919, p. 1427).

[2] We should remember that in this context work does not include executive activities.

classes'. Seen from this viewpoint they would constitute a margin in respect of the classes of the ideal dichotomy. In this context the word 'margin' has no quantitative connotation. Depending on the structure of different societies the grouping corresponding to this margin can be larger than one of the basic classes or even than either of them.

## TYPES OF INTERPRETATION OF CLASS STRUCTURE

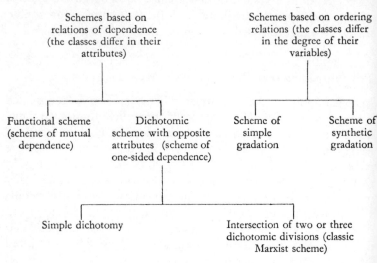

*Interpretation of the Demand for Equality amongst the Unequal*

Amongst the schemes of social structure examined was that of the non-egalitarian society without a class stratification. Just as the Marxist image of capitalist society expresses the tendency to lay the maximum emphasis on the importance of class divisions, so the image of a non-egalitarian classless society marks the extreme of the opposite tendency. This view of society takes into account all the criteria of a 'class' society which were discussed in Chapter IX and also the criteria concerning the sharpness of class boundaries considered in Chapter VI.

The co-presence of the ideal of equality with hierarchical tendencies has, as we have seen, a long tradition. In contrast to the sort of equality envisaged by the authors of *La Conjuration de Égaux* in the years 1795–6, the principle of equality amongst the gentry in the old Polish Republic or the principle of civic equality in Athens, are concerned with equality amongst the unequal, as is the principle of universal equality on the banners of the French Revolution, in the American Creed and in the Soviet Constitution.

Attempts to find a more precise definition of this sort of equality, which has to be reconciled with the maintenance of inequality between individuals, have usually run into difficulties. At one time it was suggested that what was meant was equality with respect to all man-made privileges combined with the maintenance only of 'natural inequalities'. It appeared, however, that not only 'natural inequalities', that is to say, of physical strength and abilities, were involved, but also inequalities of social status, inequalities which could at best be explained and justified as arising out of 'natural inequalities'. Then came an interpretation in terms of political equality in contradistinction to economic equality, but this could not be acceptable to an ideology in which political institutions are only the super-structure over an economic base. Moreover, even in the American Creed, the equality which is intended to characterize American society is something more than political equality.

Here we are concerned, not with the fact that these demands for equality are not demands for equality in every respect, but with a different aspect. According to the democratic demands just considered, people are equal if the inequalities between them do not constitute the criterion for membership of distinct social categories, if they do not form the basis for divisions into groups close to the model of a social class which I attempted to outline in the last chapter.

In my view, the term 'non-egalitarian classlessness' used in the two final chapters of the first part of this study refers to the concept with which these demands are concerned; and it seems to me that it is precisely this concept which affords the easiest explanation of the sense of that kind of demand for equality which has to be reconciled with an extensive range of social statuses and of shares in the national income, and which even makes allowance for combating the tendency to level-off these shares. In a class-system the simplest indicator of the relationships of equality and inequality is afforded by class barriers; the members of one class are in the same respect equal with each other,[1]

[1] Cf. Goblot: 'La barrière et le niveau, Paris, 1925.

and in the same respect unequal in relation to members of other classes. The egalitarian principle in the French Revolution, in the American Declaration of Independence and in modern Soviet ideology accepts only such inequalities among people – even if this involves very extensive economic inequality – as would, not, according to the accepted assumptions in these societies, afford a basis for the division of the citizens into separate basic groups. To put this another way, what is involved here is the abolition of inequalities described in terms of class differences, combined with the retention of inequalities of social status and economic privileges as applied to individuals. In this connexion the abolition of class privileges and discriminations can be conceived in various ways. For a French bourgeois living in the days of Enfantin and Guizot it would have consisted in the abolition of legally-enforced 'estate' norms and in the introduction of equal political rights; at the time of the French Revolution the democratization of *mores* was also involved, a process of which the outward sign was to be the use of the title *citoyen*. For the ideologists of the Soviet Union and the people's democracies, the removal of class inequalities consists in attaining uniform relations to the means of production.

In Chapters VI and VII, I introduced the concept of non-egalitarian classlessness, not in connexion with an analysis of ideological demands, but with definite ways of viewing some concrete societies. As we have seen, the objective reality with which these ways of viewing are concerned may impose an interpretation which is very far removed from that which a classless society would require. But from the viewpoint of the interests of privileged and ruling groups the utility of presenting one's own society in terms of a non-egalitarian classless society is apparent. In the world of today, both in the *bourgeois* democracies and the people's democracies, such a presentation affords no bases for group solidarity amongst the underprivileged; it inclines them to endeavour to improve their fortunes, and to seek upward social mobility by means of personal effort and their own industry, and not by collective action.

In estate or caste societies belief in the classlessness of one's own estate or caste strengthens the latter's cohesiveness and solidarity in relation to other estates or castes. An instance of the practical consequences resulting from propagating such a belief in a caste society may be sought in the long-established one-party system in the Southern States, in the homeland of American democr*v* y. The white South still remembers how the appearance of the class-based Populist Party at the end of the nineteenth century under-mined the solidarity of the white population and threatened white supremacy, when the contesting parties began to seek Negro voters.

# Chapter XI

## SEMANTIC CONVENTIONS CONSIDERED AS SOCIAL FACTS

*Definitions and Propositions*[1]

MY ANALYSIS of the various ways of interpreting social structure in the last chapter makes it clear that different concepts of social class correspond to different schemes of class system. The differences of opinion were concerned with the type of relations which should determine a class system. In treating these differences of opinion as differences in the meaning of the term 'class', we assume that the definition of a social class takes into account not only this class's inclusion in a system of basic groups, but also the type of relations on which this inclusion is to depend: that is to say, that the definition of social class in its more general sense should indicate whether the classes are components of a system of gradation, whether they are antagonistic groups, or, finally, whether they are groups differentiated in respect of their functions in the process of production.

Such an assumption is, however, by no means necessary. In Chapter IX I was endeavouring to find a common conceptual content in different definitions of social class. In this way a more general concept emerged, the concept of basic groups in the social structure, these groups being characterized by three or four conditions which were usually tacitly accepted. If this concept of basic groups in the social structure is taken to constitute the *genus proximum,* the various definitions of social class introduce

[1] The term 'proposition' as used in this study means 'declarative sentence formulated in some particular language'. I shall be using 'proposition' and 'statement' as synonymous terms.

particular *differentias specificas* which in one way or another narrow down the extensions of the concept of basic groups and lead to the different concepts of social class. One can however interpret these definitions in yet another way. In practice the so-called definitions often turn out to be propositions about a concept which is introduced without a definition. Alleged definitions of social class may be propositions about the concept of social class, a concept which is identified with that concept of the basic group in the social structure which was to constitute the *genus proximum*. The true nature of such apparent definitions is sometimes revealed quite clearly in subsequent polemical exchanges.

By way of illustration we may take the simplified 'definition' of a social class as a group determined by its relation to the means of production. In the first interpretation we should understand such a statement in roughly the following manner: 'A social class is a component of such a system of basic groups in a social structure in which its position is determined by its relation to the means of production'. In a second interpretation this statement would take another form: 'Every social class, that is to say, every group which is a component of a system of basic groups in a social structure, is determined by its relation to the means of production.'

The situation is similar if one accepts the assumption that the division of society into classes is the most important division; the most important whether because of the variety of social processes conditioned by this division or because of the role of social class membership in shaping the lives and psychological dispositions of individuals. An assumption of this kind can fulfil the functions of a definition, but then such apparent definitions as: 'social classes are groups determined by their relation to the means of production' or: 'classes are groups in which marriages contracted within the group prevail'[1] become statements about reality; the subject of these statements, that is, 'social class', is used in an 'intuitive' meaning, in a meaning established in a previous context imprecisely and without a clear-cut definition.

When Marx took ownership of the means of production and the employment of hired labour as criteria for the class division, he did not regard this as the introduction of a new concept of class

---

[1] This is more or less Schumpeter's 'a suitable definition of class', cited in Ch. IX above. This writer is also under the misapprehension that a 'definition' of this kind involves no class theory.

but as the discovery of an important law, as the comprehension of the essential nature of class divisions. The writings of Marx and his followers imply clearly that they ascribed the statements about the nature of social class made by other writers with whom they disagreed not to the ambiguity of the term 'class' but to lack of knowledge about reality; later they even ascribed such statements to a deliberate desire to mislead people. Similarly, those contemporary American sociologists who adhere to the psychological criterion of social class agree on the psychological interpretation of 'social class' not because they subscribe to the same semantic convention but because they are in agreement with a certain statement. This is the statement that the divisions of society that are most important for the system of social relations are those which are dominant in the consciousness of its members. In 1893, Bryce stated that in America – unlike Europe – society should not be divided into upper and lower, or richer and poorer classes, but that the classes should be differentiated according to their occupations.[1] Although Bryce's statement is directed against the familiar definitions of the concept of class of the type on which the scheme of gradation is based, we can have no doubt that here he was not putting forward semantic suggestions but a proposition which made use of a wider intuitive concept of class and which referred to the American reality of his day.

## Three Viewpoints concerning Semantic Conventions

We encounter three viewpoints about the discrepancies in the meaning of the terms which appear in academic and journalistic writing. All three are particularly noticeable in the sphere of sociological problems.

The first viewpoint is one which we may call 'prelogical'. Here no differentiation is made between statements giving information about the meaning of a word and statements about its designata. It is assumed that there are true and false definitions of terms in regard to the characteristics of their designata and that the meaning of terms cannot be established by an arbitrary convention. From this viewpoint, Marxist philosophers were, until recently, in the habit of reproaching those who studied semantic problems or

---

[1] J. Bryce, *The American Commonwealth*, Vol II. Macmillan and Co. 1893, p. 297. H. Lasswell and A. Kaplan, *Power and Society*, Yale University Press 1950, p. 66.

made statements concerned with the meaning of words and not with the characteristics of objects for adopting an idealistic attitude to reality.

Opposed to the first viewpoint is the logical viewpoint which clearly differentiates between statements about the meaning of words and statements about their designata. In accordance with the principles of logic we treat a definition either as a normative statement (in projecting definitions) entirely unconcerned with truth and falsity, or as a statement letting us know how certain words are actually used, and thus as a statement the truth or falsity of which depends on no phenomena other than the use of these words in such a way and not another way by certain people in certain situations. This will be clear to everyone who is familiar with the methods of scholarly work and does not confuse the symbol with the object symbolised. In 'Romeo and Juliet', even the youthful Juliet is quite aware of the conventional character of names:

> 'What's in a name? that which we call a rose
> By any other name would smell as sweet.'

But even when we understand the function of a definition in this manner, particularly when we treat projecting definitions as the outcome of an arbitrary convention, it is possible to consider the definitions in various ways and to evaluate in different ways the statements of those whose viewpoint we have characterised as pre-logical. Thus we may draw a distinction between two viewpoints which are held by those who regard a projecting definition as a matter of convention. These viewpoints we may ascribe to the 'logician' and to the 'sociologist', putting these terms in inverted commas because we are treating them only as arbitrarily chosen symbols for certain patterns of personality. It would probably be possible to establish statistically that the logician's profession inclines him to treat phenomena in a more abstract way than does that of the sociologist. But this does not mean that the viewpoints which we have distinguished should be determined by the professions of logician or sociologist respectively.

The difference between the 'logician's' viewpoint and that of the 'sociologist' is above all one of fields of interest. The 'logician' is interested only in the meaning of a defining statement. For the 'sociologist' a definition is some kind of a social fact, and he is interested in the views and inclinations which it expresses. The 'logician' depersonalizes the procedure of defining, while the 'sociologist' endeavours to get some insight into the intentions of the person who makes the statement. The 'logician' maintains that definitions tell us about conventions referring to the suggested meaning of words (projecting definitions) or about the ways in which particular words are really understood by those who use them (these I call reporting definitions); in the second case he often forgets to make it quite clear to which milieu the reporting definition is related. Nor does he take into account the possibility that definitions may indirectly tell us about certain views held by the person who is making the definition regarding the designata of the definiendum or regarding the objects which are connected in one way or another with the designata.

Differences of interests involve a different attitude to the 'prelogical viewpoint' and here we are concerned not only with the question of interests but with a difference of opinions. The 'logician' regards statements made from the 'prelogical viewpoint' about 'false' and 'true' definitions as nonsensical, and disputes about the meaning of words which are not concerned with psychological facts (i.e. in what way certain individuals or groups understand certain words) as meaningless. The 'sociologist' is in agreement with those who hold the 'prelogical viewpoint' that controversies about the meaning of words, about the way in which certain words should be understood, controversies in which the opponents are seeking objective criteria, need not be meaningless. The 'sociologist' recognises that the 'prelogical viewpoint' is based on a pertinent though unhappily expressed insight: in the humanities and the social sciences semantic conventions are not usually neutral in relation to material problems; semantic differences are usually a symptom of differences which reach into the core of the matter.

Marxist criticisms of Western European views regarding the problems of definitions were the outcome of a primitive kind of misunderstanding. They do however contain a valid idea which the conventionalists often fail to perceive. In the differences of conceptual apparatus the Marxist rightly perceives mutually exclusive views, but he does not look for these where they are actually to be found. Instead he seeks them wrongly in the formulations of differently conceived definitions – and not in the assumptions which govern the choice from among differing conceptions of definition.

*Terminological Divergences and Conceptual Differences*

When discussing in Chapter VIII the history of the relationship between the term 'class' and the term 'estate' I tried to find an explanation for a certain fairly common ambiguity in the meaning of the term 'class'. I established three denotations of this term, the widest of which comprised the other two. I then pointed out that when speaking or writing of problems of social structure the same persons may use this term in a more general meaning at one time and in a less general meaning at another, and that this sometimes happens because they do not clearly realize this ambiguity, owing to the fact that the content of the narrower concept is reflected in the wider one. At other times it is the context that modifies the meaning of the term 'class' and then there is no fear of misunderstandings.

In academic works this ambiguity can be cleared up by consistent adherence to a particular definition; but because the definitions made by different writers clear up the ambiguity in various ways, differences of meaning appear between the terminology used in different studies. For example, when Sorokin defined social class he emphasized that he was referring to the kind of group that is particularly characteristic of Western European societies of the eighteenth, nineteenth and twentieth centuries.[1] Lasswell and Kaplan, on the other hand, definied class so broadly that estates and castes were included in the extension of this concept.[2]

In the construction of sociological theories of class, the distinction of concepts has in some cases entailed terminological distinctions in other respects than that concerned with the threefold denotation about which we have spoken; the terms 'stratum' and 'estate' (the latter no longer being used in the historical sense) have at times been introduced in addition to the term 'class', and definite meanings have been established for them. But even then the conventions made by different authors do not accord with one another, the same word designating different concepts. For

---

[1] *Society, Culture and Personality*, New York, 1947, p. 271.
[2] *op. cit.*, pp. 62–64.

instance, 'social stratum' may be opposed to 'social class' either with reference to a different principle of dividing society into basic groups, as has been done by Centers or Touraine,[3] or with reference to its greater divergence from the model of social class, as in Marxist theory.[2] When Weber introduced a distinction between class and estate (*der Ständ*), he conceived of a class as a group whose membership is determined exclusively by objective economic criteria. On the other hand, the 'psychological' concept of a class used by Centers and other contemporary American sociologists[3] (and which, according to Centers is opposed to the concept of a stratum based on 'objective' criteria) is closer in meaning to Weber's 'estate'. When we speak of the divergences and misunderstandings in sociological terminology, when we draw attention to terminological misunderstandings in a discussion, or contrast differing definitions of such terms as 'class' or 'social stratum', for instance as they are used by the Marxists, Pareto, Tönnies, Max Weber, T. H. Marshall, or the American sociologists, we may be concerned either with terminological divergencies or with conceptual differences.

Terminological differences occur when we are employing the same concepts but refer to them by means of different and translatable terms. For instance, Adam Smith called his three basic groups in the social structure 'orders', while Marx, when he accepted Adam Smith's division in the third volume of *Das Kapital*, called the same groups the three basic 'classes'. Here we are dealing with a difference of terminology only. I would also include in the category of terminological differences the sort of case in which the same term designates different concepts, so long as the conceptual contents are sufficiently distinct for the term by which they are referred to in common not to constitute any link between them. In such cases we realize that the common term is not due to the intersection of the extension of the respective concepts, but has its origin in chance. Such an example is the differing use of the identical term 'social stratum' by Marxist writers and Centers.

[1] Cf. Ch. III.

[2] 'Stratum' – conceived of as a group similar to a social class but insufficiently cohesive or possessing the essential attributes to an insufficient degree. Cf. Chapters IV and VI.

[3] 'Class, as distinguished from stratum, can well be regarded as a psychological phenomenon in the fullest sense of the term.' Centers, *op. cit.*, p. 27.

A second and far more important category of the differences we are considering is to be found in situations where the same term refers to different concepts with similar but not identical extensions. Here the use of the same term is accounted for by the fact that the most representative designata of the one and the other concept are common to both.

The majority of social anthropologists and students of the psychology of religion define religion, in line with everyday notions, as a set of rituals and beliefs concerning relations to supernatural beings. For Durkheim and his school, however, religion is a set of practices and beliefs, which are obligatory in a given community under the sanction of universal condemnation. Here the extensions of the two concepts designated by the same term 'religion' are not identical. Durkheim's concept would embrace 'atheistic religion' as well as others, while from the other viewpoint 'atheistic religion' is a *contradictio in adjecto*. On the other hand the Durkheimian definition would not apply to individual religious beliefs, because in this case religion always requires a church, an assembly of the faithful. Thus the extensions of the two concepts designated by the term 'religion' do not coincide; nevertheless all religions *par excellence* (*par excellence* from one and from the other viewpoint) fall within the two extensions.

Moreover, it was these most typical kinds of religion that provided the material whose analysis produced both these definitions. The reason why Durkheim included 'atheistic religions' in the extension of his concept and excluded uninstitutionalized religions from it was because, in his analysis of these religions *par excellence*, he recognized the significance of other factors than did Leuba or Malinowski; this inclined him to correct the traditional boundaries of the designata accordingly. The particular characteristics of the typical religions which the Durkheimian school considered as most socially significant made it necessary for them to include in the same category certain systems of practices and beliefs which are not connected with the worship of any divine being. Freud, on the other hand, regarded personal relations and the transference of relations characteristic of the family as the most important element in religious beliefs, and he would not have regarded such an extension of the concept of religion as appropriate. Thus by extending or narrowing down the scope of the phenomena falling under a common category we change the manner in which they are perceived.

## The Background of Conceptual Differences

Durkheim's concept of religion – to return to this example – is undoubtedly an expression of the French sociologists' interest in the problems of the social bond. On the other hand, a psychologist – who is interested in the influence of belief in a supernatural world on the psychological attitudes of the individual – or a student of the history of religious myths and their role in artistic creativeness would conceive of the phenomena under investigation in terms of different conceptual categories. Here we should also be dealing with different views about the origin of religions, and thus with different views about reality, and finally with different social tendencies. Durkheim's concept of religion can also be associated with the efforts to strengthen the social bond in the atomized France of his day, and with the endeavour to oppose simultaneously the extreme individualism of that period and the claims of the Catholic Church, which itself wished to provide the social cement for the French nation. In all this Durkheim's concept of religion afforded the prospect of finding a 'secular' bond which could fulfil 'religious functions'.

During this study we have frequently encountered the striking fact that different concepts of social class reveal different theories of social life, distinct ideologies and differing codes of conduct. But when we came across different concepts of class in the work of one writer, we attributed this either to the variety of the problems involved or to the way in which practical problems change in different circumstances. For instance, when, in considering the Stalinist concept of the 'non-antagonistic class' we maintained that the term 'social class' as used in the Soviet Union had changed its meaning in relation to Lenin's definition, we were interested not so much in the terminology and conceptual apparatus applied by Soviet writers as in the images of the country's social structure and the ideological standpoint that was reflected in these conceptual changes.

The relationship between the choice of conceptual apparatus and the choice of problems is perfectly clear and in general arouses no doubts. Less obvious, however, is the relationship between the choice of concepts and statements about reality. The conceptual apparatus to a certain extent predetermines the scope of the problems. On the other hand, one or another way of framing concepts does not predetermine the statements which can be formulated by means of these concepts; the same concepts could be employed for contradictory propositions. In this respect the conventionalists are correct in saying that concepts are neutral with respect to incompatible statements.

But a deliberate formation of concepts or a deliberate acceptance of some and rejection of others is a purposeful activity – we can ask about its aims. To fix the boundaries of the application of concepts in a particular way can be the result of a passive submission to tradition, but it can also be the result of choice. Disputes over the boundaries of concepts are – provided one does not assume a prelogical standpoint – disputes about the relative importance of particular boundaries. This is the case with differences of opinion concerned with the extension of the concepts of social class or religion. Methodological controversies concerned with the extension of concepts of history since Dilthey's time can serve as another example.

If both opposing parties are concerned with the same sort of importance, a difference in their viewpoints may be the result of a disagreement of opinion about certain causal relationships. For example, they may disagree as to which is the more important factor in the social bond: to take a rural population in an as yet unurbanized environment, is it the way of life and cultural traditions or the uniform relation to the means of production? The first instance would involve recognizing the existence of a peasant class; in the second, the collectivity of peasants would be divided up by class boundaries determined according to different criteria. But if – as is usually the case – one of the disputants has in mind a different kind of importance from the other, the differences of viewpoints originate in differing value-scales and practical directives; this does not of course exclude the possibility of a disagreement of opinions as to causal relationships as well.

## The Motives of Disputes over Terms

Seen from the viewpoint of the frame of the definition, the procedure of defining may perform different functions. It may be governed either by purely terminological interests, when it is a matter of choosing a term for a concept that has already been previously established and verbalized, or by conceptual interests, when one is concerned with establishing the extension of the concept which one desires to designate by means of such and such a word. An example of the first kind of defining is the adoption of new terms in physics, or the method applied by Pareto in his sociological system. The latter would first associate a letter of the alphabet with the concept which he had constructed, so as to free it from all association with colloquial speech; only later, for convenience' sake, would he replace this letter by some term taken from everyday language.

This whole discussion of the background of differences in choosing ways of communicating with one another has been concerned only with conceptual differences. Where the choice of terms is concerned, however, the situation would on the face of it seem to be different and terminological differences would indeed appear to be only a question of arbitrary conventions. The choice of the concepts to be used and the boundaries of their extension do to a certain extent determine the problem-matter and exert some influence in other ways on one's process of thinking. But the same intellectual processes can be carried on by means of different terms. They can also be carried on in different languages, so long as each language can be exactly translated into the other.

While all this is true, the terms themselves are not however necessarily neutral, particularly when problems of the humanities and the social sciences are concerned. The main reason for this is of course the propaganda value of certain words. Everyone realizes how important the selection of words is for political speeches or writing. Particular words have a particular sphere of associations and some have acquired a formidable emotional charge, whether positive or negative. In view of practical requirements and consequences it is not a matter of indifference to which designata these emotional values and associations are attributed. The emotional value of words was discussed by Charles Stevenson in connection with his concept of 'persuasive definitions'.[1] He distinguished between the 'descriptive meaning' and the 'emotive

---

[1] Charles L. Stevenson: *Ethics and Language*, Yale University Press, (6th ed. 1953). Chapter IX.

meaning' of words.[1] I should however prefer to use the term 'meaning' in a narrower sense and to distinguish between the 'meaning' of words and their 'emotional charge', or the emotional quality connected with the expressive function of words.

The use of the term 'religion' in Durkheim's sense has been strongly opposed by both the Catholics and the Marxists – but for different reasons. For the Catholics, as for other religious groups, the word 'religion' is a term of respect referring to the supreme values, and they do not wish to share it with atheistic groups. Nor do they wish to admit that in the concept of religion emphasis should be put on pressure by the church and the intolerance of believers. For the Marxists, on the other hand, the term 'religion' has a negative quality. The Durkheimian use of the term would allow Marxism to be included in the concept of a religion, which in the Marxist milieu is conceived of as an opiate for the masses. Clearly Marxists would not wish to be associated in any way with such a concept, nor to be classified in the same category as the religious churches, which they regard as instruments of the exploiting classes and survivals from the dark past of superstition. The idea of performing a 'religious function' would be much easier for Marxists to accept if it were differently named.

An emotional charge of another kind is connected with the word 'class'. In the conventional sense it would be possible to substitute the term 'stratum' for the term 'class'. But as a signal for conditioned reflexes the term 'stratal enemy' would hardly take the place of 'class enemy'. The social functions of the term 'nation' have also made the Communist Party anxious to confer this name on the Negroes in the United States, although this attribution does not accord with the Stalinist definition of a nation as generally accepted by the Communist Party.

Again, the use of the terms 'socialism' and 'communism' in the so-called Stalinist period seemed to some people, and especially to those who had fought for socialism before World War II, some sort of profanation of words which had a high emotional value for them. Such people were reluctant to confer the name of 'socialist countries' to the countries of Eastern Europe. In 1957 I attended a youth club meeting in Warsaw at which some of the members asked whether it would not be better to abandon the word socialism, which because of its recent associations was thought to

[1] *Ibid.*, Chs. III and IV.

have become ambiguous and ambivalent, or to preserve it as the name of the social order towards which they were aiming, to purify its meaning and to preserve the emotional charge originally attached to this word. Most of the club members who had not lost their faith in socialist ideas wished to preserve the name – they would not in fact have agreed with Juliet's sentiment about the rose.

We are all familiar with the role played by the term 'democracy' in the ideological disputes between East and West. The word has a positive tinge in both opposing camps in the modern world. Again, while the term 'metaphysics' has one meaning for the Marxists[1] and another for the positivists, it is pejorative in both cases. The Marxists are opposed to the positivist interpretation of this term because it would permit the inclusion of dialectical materialism in metaphysics. There are many terms which have a differing emotional colouring in different milieux, as a result of differing traditions. In such cases they become signals which trigger off different conditioned reflexes in different milieux. The Marxists use the term 'idealism' as an offensive weapon in discussions with their adversaries, and do not always trouble overmuch about its meaning in concrete contexts. When the Professor of Philosophy at Wilno University, Wincenty Lutoslawski, began his conflict with the Marxists forty years ago, he turned their own slogan, the term 'materialism', against them as a weapon, saying with contempt: 'They themselves can hardly deny that they are materialists'.

Particular terms with a suitable tradition may sometimes be used as working tools when operating with conceptual amalgams. We speak of the latter when two or three denotations which are different but have certain similarities are involved in the meaning of a word. Conceptual amalgams, though disastrous in theoretical analyses, can be very convenient for propaganda purposes, as I said earlier. Hence the resistance which follows attempts to establish a uniform sense for such terms as 'a scientific law', 'labour', 'history' or 'race'. For certain purposes it is convenient to use the term 'law', which in one sense means a statement of the invariable sequence of events occurring in specified conditions formulated by an individual scientist (e.g. Newton's Law, the Boyle-Mariotte Law, etc.), in another the forces of

[1] Cf. F. Engels, *Anti-Dühring*, London, Lawrence & Wishart, 1934, p. 27.

nature that govern this sequence of events or the natural regularities which constitute the matter of laws in the first meaning ('the inexorable laws of history' in the Marxist interpretation). Leaders of political or religious movements often show a marked reluctance to accept attempts made to establish the precise meaning of words. Ambiguous, vague and obscure terms can be useful in politics because they lend themselves to different interpretations in changing conditions. Even as early as the fourth century A.D., during the struggle against the Arian heresy, most of the bishops were decidedly unwilling to support Ambrosius in his attempt to give the exact meaning of some of the doctrinal terms used by the Church. And in our century, Alfred Rosenberg, a leading Nazi theorist, declared that it was indecent to go too far in analysing the concept of race.

I have spent some time in discussing the propaganda functions of terms since they are the most striking. But propaganda value is not the only matter involved when we are concerned with the relationship between the choice of terms and the view of reality. The choice of a particular term, even when it is made with full awareness that this is a matter of convention, may be the expression of certain views about reality, while a terminological difference may reflect incompatible statements. Certain words which have been associated in a special way with important matters have acquired a significance which other words lack. The concept to which such a word refers achieves a higher position in the hierarchy of conceptual importance ('importance' is not here understood in terms of the level of abstraction of concepts). And it is for this reason that when controversies arise about the boundaries of application of the concepts which are to be designated by such terms as 'religion', 'art', 'scientific law' and 'social class', it is impossible to separate terminological differences from conceptual ones.

In a controversy about the denotation of the term 'religion' involving the designation of two different concepts by the same name, there is from a theoretical standpoint nothing to stop the opponents from reaching an agreement on terminology, whereby this term will be reserved for one of the two competing concepts and the other concept will be referred to by another arbitrarily chosen term. But the term which has already acquired significance will enhance the importance of the scope of application of the concept which is to be designated by this term. And this – apart from propaganda considerations – can exert some influence on the construction and interpretation of a theory even after the various terminological misunderstandings have been clarified. The belief that a particular logical distinction is an essential distinction is responsible for the fact that the terms which are applied to it assume particular importance for us. But the association between the importance of the distinction and the importance of the term works in the opposite direction as well. The belief that we are dealing with an important term usually suggests that the distinction which corresponds to this term is a fundamental distinction, and that the characteristics of the phenomena and the causal relationships thus distinguished in this way are especially significant. In accordance with this assumption, the adoption of such terms as 'religion' or 'art' in a particular manner constitutes an expression of a particular view about cultural phenomena. One such view might be that which holds that problems concerned with the pressure of any socially-sanctioned dogmas of any kind are more important than problems concerned with differences in the social functions of theism and atheism; and that the first set of problems therefore deserve precedence in certain areas of theory construction.[1]

For the purpose of theory construction as well as for propaganda considerations, it is not immaterial whether we agree on a convention to refer to the different *strata* of the peasant *class*, or to speak of the different *classes* of the peasant *stratum*. Long-established associations have given the term 'class' a different value for us in theory construction than the term 'stratum', and have caused the boundaries between classes to be drawn with a heavier line than the boundaries of strata. This function of certain terms is not exclusively confined to the domain of the humanities and social sciences, and it would be possible to find analogies in the terminology of the natural sciences.

Attempts have been made to neutralise sociological terms, and to oppose the loading of terms with a ballast of associations and emotions. Amongst the earliest of these were the heuristic procedures applied by Pareto in his *Traité de sociologie*. For the moment, however, we are not concerned with this particular question. In comparing differing theoretical and ideological standpoints in the

---

[1] The reference in this passage is to Durkheim's theory of religion.

domain of sociological problems, we have constantly had to deal with terms which are not neutral; for this reason it is not only in the choice of concepts but also in the choice of terms that we are confronted with the problem of concealed assumptions and views about the importance of particular matters for the whole system of social relations.

There are many seemingly factual controversies in which people attack not views but words, without realizing that they are not speaking the same language, and sometimes even without properly understanding the meaning of their own words themselves. This kind of controversy can be resolved by means of semantic clarifications, which will show that the controversy was spurious or that its point was to be found elsewhere.

On the other hand, a dispute over words is not usually simply a dispute about words, even when both sides believe that the matter at issue merely concerns the choice of means by which a thought is to be formulated. If, in such situations, we wish to understand the essential difference between the standpoints involved in the dispute, we should seek this in their incompatible views about reality or in their divergent aims.

# Chapter XII

## INTERPRETATIONS OF CLASS STRUCTURE IN HISTORICAL PERSPECTIVE

*Views of Class Structure and their Denotata*

OUR ANALYSIS of different kinds of materials has led us to distinguish several basic ways of interpreting class structure; I tried to present these in a systematic form in Chapter X.

Interpretations of class structure are social facts, which constitute a response to the emergence or persistence of certain types of human relationships. Thus the typology of the modes of interpreting such structures may be correlated with the typology of the actual structures. When we are dealing with class structures this correlation of schemes with the object interpreted is a rather complicated problem, but the materials which we have been considering do allow us to distinguish at least three possible solutions:

1. Sometimes one author will apply different schemes in describing the same society. Here I am referring not only to instances resulting from a change of views (as may have happened in the case of St. John Chrysostom) but also to cases where a writer uses different schemes – because he is considering different aspects of the social structure. This can apply both to theoreticians when they are considering different problems, and to men of action, when they are justifying successive points in their programmes. In Aristotle's *Politics*[1] we find at least four different views of the class structure of the Greek city-states of his day.

[1] See pp. 40, 42.

In addition to his basic division into freemen and slaves, Aristotle presents another fundamental dichotomy of opposite attributes by dividing the whole population into those who work and those who do not work. At times one even has the impression that he regards this division as more important than the division into freemen and slaves.[1]

In the same work we find a trichotomous scheme of gradation[2] and a functional conception of social structure, with the population divided into several categories, each of which has distinct and important functions to perform for the society as a whole. With Marx, as we have seen, all the schemes of social structure which we have considered intersect in his interpretations of contemporary society.

2. The second kind of correlation arises when a writer employs different schemes in relation to different societies or to different social systems which are mutually opposed. In such cases the application of different schemes is supposed to result from the differences which exist between the objects described. For example, at the end of the nineteenth century Bryce, wishing to oppose the two societies, applied one scheme of social structure to the United States and another to the capitalist countries of Western Europe.[3] A similar but far more fundamental and radical approach is used by contemporary Marxists when they contrast the class structure of the Soviet Union with the social relationships prevailing in the United States or the capitalist countries of Western Europe.

3. The third possibility is the application of different schemes to the same society, made by the representatives of different milieux who disagree as to the true character of this society. An example of this possibility may be found in the interpretation of contemporary American society in terms of a scheme of gradation or a scheme of non-egalitarian classlessness, or in the Marxist interpretation, the choice of interpretation depending on the beliefs of the writer. Another example might be the various ways of conceiving contemporary Soviet society: in terms of a functional scheme, as applied by Soviet scholars, and in terms of a scheme of

[1] *Ibid.*, Bk. III, Ch. V.
[2] 'In every city the people are divided into three sorts; the very rich, the very poor, and those who are between them.' *Politics*, Bk. IV, Ch. XI.
[3] *op. cit.*, Vol. II. p. 297.

gradation, as applied by Russian *emigré* writers and some American sociologists. Looking further into the past, we may refer to the contrast discussed in Chapter IV between the dichotomic view of mediaeval society and the functional interpretation propagated by the Church (the division of the population into those who pray, those who defend the country and those who work). Such differences of approach can be explained by differences of 'class perspective'. I have already referred to these differences of perspective in the cases of Babeuf and Saint-Simon, each of whom saw the fundamental division of society running along quite different lines, and in the entirely different meaning attached to the metaphor of the bees by Saint-Simon and Shelley, although in this case all three writers made use of the same dichotomic scheme. The differences in class perspective were conditioned by the fact that Babeuf or Shelley felt a solidarity with different strata of the same society than did Saint-Simon and his followers.

It is not however merely a question of perspective. The particular interpretations of class structure which are symbolically expressed by various schemes or by different versions of the same scheme – as in the case of Babeuf and Saint-Simon – suggest different practical policies. We have noted how those who defend the existing social order, whether it be Agrippa, Theodoret, Spencer or Stalin, are inclined to present the structure of their own society in terms of a functional scheme or one of non-egalitarian classlessness.[1] Revolutionaries, on the other hand, tend to view the world in terms of a dichotomy with opposite attributes. It can also happen, however, that the same scheme lends itself for application by two opposing social tendencies. In Chapter II I discussed situations in which the representatives of the privileged class employ the same scheme of social structure as do the representatives of the under-privileged class. The same assumptions and the same interpretations of phenomena can in fact serve mutually exclusive purposes and I tried in that chapter to formulate the conditions which appear to favour such a case.

The choice of a particular scheme of class structure may also be connected with the evaluation of the importance of the class division in general; this evaluation depends in turn on this 'class perspective' and on the social programme of those making the

[1] Cf. Chapters III, VII, VIII above.

evaluation. The question of the class division assumes one kind of significance in the eyes of the under-privileged class and quite another in the eyes for instance, of members of the Oxford Group, who maintained that the only important thing is not whether one lives in a cottage or a palace, but purity of heart. We have seen what role Marx's belief in the immense importance of class divisions played in his conception of social class. We have also noted that in this respect too we can contrast the Marxian conception not only with American interpretations of the structure of American society but also with the Stalinist conception of classes in the Soviet Union.

The three fundamental possibilities listed above, possibilities in which we are dealing with different schemes of class structure, can be presented in the form of a diagram. The letter O stands for the observer who is interpreting the social structure, and the letter S for the social structure or the type of social order interpreted.

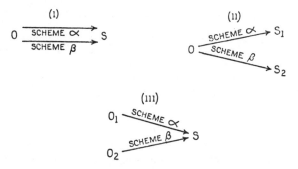

A special case of differences in interpretations occurs when the second and third types of possibility are combined: that is to say, when representatives of different social milieux not only interpret the structure of the same society differently but when each of them applies the same scheme to the other of two structurally different societies which are regarded as mutually opposed in this respect, as is the case with the United States and the Soviet Union.

## *The Choice of a Viewpoint or the Description of the Denotata*

In the preceding chapter I discussed the relationship between the choice of conceptual apparatus and the theoretical and practical viewpoint regarding the reality to which this apparatus is to be applied. One of my objects was to establish the origins of conceptual and terminological disputes about sociological problems; and the question of applying a particular scheme of class structure in the description of actual societies or historical types of social order is a particular instance of that wider problem.

From this review of the types of correlation between different ways of viewing social structure and their denotata we may now say that the choice of a scheme of class structure in a particular instance is symptomatic either of the problems which interest those who apply the scheme or of their views on the reality which they are describing.

As we have seen, it is possible to apply the majority, if not all, of the schemes we have been considering to almost every class society. Different conceptual categories correspond to different problems. By conceiving a social structure in terms of a particular scheme, we confer a particular aspect on the social structure. Depending on the kind of problem in which one is interested, one can interpret the same society in terms of a dichotomic scheme, of a scheme of gradation, or of a functional scheme; or, alternately, one can apply the same scheme to it in a different manner, for example by introducing different criteria of gradation or of functional divisions.

But particular schemes which are applied, to some extent arbitrarily, to a specific reality correspond to certain ideal types. Thus when we compare different societies we can indicate objective criteria in respect of which we perceive a greater or lesser distance between particular social structures and a particular ideal type, and thereby assert that a certain scheme is more suited to the one society than another. For instance, there need be no doubt that a dichotomic scheme is more suitable for describing pre-war Rumanian society than that of Norway, or for describing Tsarist Russia than the Western capitalist societies of our own times.[1] An interpretation of an estate-society as a social-status continuum would seem infinitely more paradoxical than such an interpretation of contemporary British society.

If one applies different schemes of social structure to different societies, the very choice of a scheme may fix in advance the characteristic features of the society which is to be described. We

[1] Cf. Togliatti's statement of 1 May, 1956.

apply a certain scheme not because it corresponds to one of the possible viewpoints but as a framework which characterizes a given society in contrast to certain other existing or possible societies. The application of this particular scheme is then symptomatic not of the general problems that interest us but of our view of this particular society, a view which we ourselves accept or which we wish to propagate for some practical purpose. In applying a dichotomic scheme to pre-war Rumania we can regard the dichotomy not only as one of the possible ways of viewing these societies but as a specific feature of Rumanian society in comparison with Norwegian society. This means that in our view a dichotomic scheme emphasizes more important features in the social life of pre-war Rumania than another scheme of social structure would do; or else that the features which it emphasizes were more important in the social life of Rumania than in that of Norway.

We have still to indicate the viewpoint from which we are evaluating the importance of these particular features, and the criteria of this evaluation. Most frequently the viewpoint and the criteria are not specified, because we assume that the kind of importance involved is self-explanatory. In discussions outside the academic world evaluations regarding importance are not usually formulated as relative to a person or his viewpoint, nor is the relative way of viewing phenomena emphasized; this becomes evident when, for instance, the phenomena are viewed in such a manner as if the dichotomic view were to exclude a multiple class system as seen from another viewpoint, or as if class antagonisms were to exclude a functional view of the class structure.

The application of different schemes to particular societies can thus express differing interests or differing beliefs about reality. In the first case we choose a particular scheme with regard to the problems which interest us and describe the subject-matter in one way or another within the framework of this scheme. In the second case we actually characterize the subject-matter by the very choice of scheme. Different beliefs about reality will thus find expression in differing conceptions of social class or of the class-system. For example, where Soviet ideologists see two non-antagonistic classes and a 'stratum' of intelligentsia, an American sociologist or a Russian *emigré* will perceive six or ten classes as the levels of social stratification.

## CONCEPTUAL CONSTRUCTS AND SOCIAL REALITY

### *The Ideological Superstructure of Class Structures*

In this study I have often noted the striking persistence of the fundamental ways of interpreting the social structure and of certain views of the existing system of human relations. We have come across the same views of class structure in folklore, in religious myths, in the philosophic works of the ancient world, in the writings of the Fathers of the Church, in the trends of social thought in the Middle Ages, in the works of sociological pioneers of more recent centuries, in the social consciousness of the working masses in capitalist countries and in the new socialist republics, where the image of social relations that is in process of formation in different milieux, among peasants, workers and the intelligentsia, is not always in accordance with the interpretation suggested by the authorities.

The persistence over thousands of years of certain ways of interpreting class structure, through changes of social system, of forms of production and of the distribution of wealth, indicates that in the schemes analysed we are dealing with interpretations of a class-society which are concerned with problems whose topicality is not restricted to any single social order; that is to say with interpretations of a class society in the broadest sense. This testifies to the fact that we are here dealing with questions which have been of considerable importance over a long span of generations. There can be no doubt that what is involved here are enduring social ideals, with which the defenders of the existing order also have to reckon. For the underprivileged, these enduring interpretations of class structure emphasize the conflict between the existing state of affairs and the values to which they aspire.

On the other hand, approval of the existing order has somehow always developed into apologetics. There is no need to look as late as the modern bourgeois democracies for instances of this process. Such apologetic functions were being performed many centuries earlier by the myth of Ham, the myth of the origin of the four Indian castes, or the commonsense arguments of Aristotle or Lactantius.[1] In the middle of the nineteenth century George Fitzhugh, the defender of the slave system in the Southern States, even appealed in his struggle against the Northern aboli-

---

[1] Lactantius Firmianus (c. 260 – c340 A.D.), called the 'Christian Cicero', author of *Divinarum Institutionum Libri Septem* and some treatises.

tionists to the principles of Communism; he tried to demonstrate the superiority of a system of slavery from the viewpoint of Communist ideals ('to everyone according to his needs') and attacked class oppression in the 'free' states of the industrial North.[1] Equally striking in this respect have been the arguments used since the end of the nineteenth century by defenders of racial discrimination in the United States, or in the former British Empire.

Approval of the existing order, even when expressed in the most ruthless and brutal forms, has become a defensive argument in face of an ideal – an ideal which over the centuries has been extinguished and reborn, aroused people to action, taken the form of unrealizable dreams or glimmered in the mists of an afterworld, but which has always managed to emerge from the recesses of the social consciousness to disturb the existing state of affairs. The defenders of the existing order have even been forced to reckon with this ideal's invasion of the privileged ranks, whence the leaders of revolutionary movements have been recruited on more than one occasion. The content of this ideal was codified as the threefold slogan of the French Revolution – *Liberté, Egalité, Fraternité* – and was later neutralized by an appropriate interpretation. But this content is probably more ancient than the legend of the age of Saturn and the extravagances of Antisthenes' followers. It was adopted by the proletarian revolutionaries in the nineteenth century, and it was then that the revolutionary camp accepted the term 'classless society' to aid the final realization of these slogans in their full and original meaning.

This three-fold ideal confers special importance on the interpretations of social structure which have recurred for thousands of years. The scheme of gradation emphasizes the conflict of the existing order with the ideal of equality. The dichotomic scheme stresses its conflict with all three ideals of the classless society. Despite its utilitarian justifications, the functional scheme in its negative aspect (conflict of class interests combined with mutual dependence between classes), shows an inevitable conflict between the existing social mechanism and the ideal of fraternity. In its positive aspect (the co-operation of classes through their distinctive functions) the functional scheme, and also the scheme of a social-status continuum, as expressed by the defenders of the *status quo*, pay indirect tribute to those ideals, because they present

[1] *Sociology for the South or the Failure of Free Society*, Richmond, 1854.

such aspects of the existing order as do not arouse sharp opposition from those who accept the principles linked with this triple formula and the revolutionary ideal of the classless society.

In this study we have had an opportunity of observing not only the persistence of certain schemes of class structure but also the persistence, despite cultural changes, of fundamentally opposite ways of interpreting class structure and the persistence of methods of defending the existing order. These methods have been aimed either at demonstrating that the attainment of a society of free and equal men is impossible or at presenting the existing state of affairs in the least offensive way from the viewpoint of the oppressed classes.

These conflicts and these methods have recurred in societies with social orders as far removed from one another as the Roman Republic in the days of the legendary Agrippa, or those in which Lactantius or St. Augustine lived, were from the capitalist society as seen by Spencer and as reflected in the Papal encyclical *Rerum Novarum*. And in our own period the methods of justifying the combating of *uravnilovka* in the socialist republics are very reminiscent of the arguments advanced on the other side of the Atlantic to justify inequality of economic status on the grounds of the need to increase production. These arguments again have an early precedent in the writings of the Church Fathers in the third and fourth centuries.

Marxism formulated the problem of the ideological superstructure of particular formations. Study of the conceptions of class structure over centuries has shown that class-systems have an enduring ideological superstructure independent of their particular social order.

## *The Modern Model of Social Class and Recent Transformations*

In asserting the persistence of certain ways of viewing class structure in the cultural heritage of more than two thousand years, I am not echoing Solomon's dictum that 'there is nothing new under the sun'. As I emphasized in my introduction, this persistence of certain elements in our cultural heritage forms a background against which the new views, the new attitudes and the new conceptions which have emerged as a consequence of the great social transformations of the nineteenth and twentieth centuries stand out all the more distinctly. In drawing attention to these new contents we are transferring what are, in a certain sense, age-old problems to a plane of discussion where the historical character of the ways of conceiving social structure is brought out in intervals of time limited to the life-span of one or two generations.

We have already had occasion to emphasize the consequences for European theoretical thought of the formation of a new model of society in the years between the French Revolution and Marx's *Das Kapital*. This was the model of the capitalist society, seen as a society whose structure is based on social relations arising spontaneously, a society in which the only form of real power is the power of capital, and the relations of ownership are the only determinant of the system of social statuses.

The nineteenth-century conceptions of class structure became the heritage of the twentieth century, and in the processes of shaping the social consciousness the greatest role throughout the world was played by the Marxian legacy. Meanwhile, the twentieth century brought unprecedented changes in the system of social relations, changes which provided the starting-point for this study. History has not followed the road leading to the ideal types of capitalist society. Even in his time, Lenin had to introduce certain important corrections in the Marxian view of the development of capitalist society. And as events developed, the liberal writers were faced by the fact that their optimistic idea of progress had broken down and that the course of civilization was taking 'an unexpected turn'.[1] This 'unexpected turn' divides the civilization of classic capitalism from that of the two world wars, of gigantic monopolies, of socialist countries extending over vast areas of the globe, from the civilization of social planning and atomic energy.

When in the first chapter I outlined the problems to be discussed in this study, I wrote that in the new and unprecedented conditions 'one can anticipate that the conceptual categories which have sufficed for earlier generations will appear unsuitable or inadequate.' As the argument developed the opportunity emerged more than once for establishing the dependence of the conceptual apparatus on social transformations. In changed conditions the importance of conceptual categories and schemes formulated in a different system of social relations is also altered.

[1] F. A. Hayek, *The Road to Serfdom*, Routledge, London, 1944, p. 15.

The dependence of social status on the relations to the means of production has probably existed and continues to exist in all social systems which have gone beyond a primitive form of economy. But it has never been so important a factor in the system of human relations as in the legitimate countries of free-enterprise capitalism. Marx's theory of class grasped this factor of the social structure that was fundamental for this period. And Marx's criterion of the class division proved immensely fertile in the development of social theory, by helping to draw attention to hitherto unperceived facts and by encouraging profounder investigation of social processes that were taking place all the time.

In our own world the relations of ownership to the means of production are still a factor of immense significance in the formation of human relations; without the Marxian insight into social life it would be virtually impossible to conduct an incisive analysis of the changes which are taking place in the modern world. But the scope of the applicability of the Marxian criterion has undergone important changes.

The inadequacy of the classic Marxist-Leninist conception of class for analysing the social structure of countries in which the means of production have been nationalized has found one form of expression in Stalin's conception of non-antagonistic classes, and another in the discussions about the systems of privileges enjoyed by particular groups in these countries.

The Marxian criterion of social class has also lost some of its adequacy in relation to the capitalist countries. Here I am not by any means referring only to the Fascist countries, where the large-scale application of the means of compulsion structure of countries in which the principles of economic liberalism are respected. Such changes are seen at their most effective in the United States.

According to Marx and Engels the development of capitalism was to be accompanied by a rapid process of economic polarization and by the disappearance of the middle class. The envisaged polarization did not occur, but it is by no means easy to say whether the process of disappearance of the middle class predicted by Marx is actually occurring in the world's most advanced capitalist country. The old American middle class which formed so large a part of the United States population in de Tocqueville's period, and which in his view was the guarantee of American democracy, was that of the property-owners who work in their own establishments. This class has in fact shrunk rapidly, in line with Marx's prediction, although not so rapidly as might have been expected in view of the violent rate of the accumulation of capital. Simultaneously, however, a new middle class has been rising, a class of civil servants, trade union officials, local government officers, a class of technicians, white-collar workers and minor executives in the large industrial establishments.

The rapid rise of this new class shows up strikingly in statistical returns and is changing the whole social structure of the United States. In the time of de Tocqueville and Marx it was too insignificant to be differentiated as a separate class, and it was not included in the framework of the classical Marxian division. It was a marginal group. Now this marginal group among the classes of the Marxian scheme has so increased in size in contemporary America that it is impossible not to regard it as a class, especially when we consider general trends of development in the United States.[1] This new class, which has a corresponding group in the 'stratum' of non-manual white-collar workers in state and local government and in party offices in the U.S.S.R., is, it would seem, even characterized by its own social attitudes and its own subculture.[2]

Thus the answer to the question whether the Marxian forecast about the fate of the middle class is being fulfilled in the United States depends on the interpretation of the term 'middle class'; in Marx's day this term did not involve such difficulties.

[1] Some sociologists have estimated that the percentage of people who owned their own means of livelihood in the decade between 1820 and 1830 was as much as 80 per cent of the free population of the United States. Cf. K. Mayer, 'Changes in the Social Structure of the United States', *Transactions of the Third World Congress of Sociology*, Vol. III, London 1956, p. 69. The same study gives statistical data to illustrate the reduction of the former middle class and the rise of the new one in the period 1870–1954. According to Mayer the percentage of self-employed persons amongst the working population of the United States fell from 40.4 per cent in 1870 to 13.3 per cent in 1954, while the percentage decrease of farmers was from 27.1 per cent to 5.9 per cent. The percentage of wage-workers, including farm labourers, underwent little change – from 52.8 per cent in 1870 to 55.8 per cent in 1954. On the other hand the percentage of salaried employees (in contrast to wage-workers) grew from 6.6 per cent in 1870 to 30.8 per cent in 1954: within this group the percentage of civil servants and clerical workers rose from 0.6 per cent in 1870 to 13.1 per cent in 1954 (*op. cit.*, p. 70).

[2] Cf. L. Corey: *The Middle Class* in *Class, Status and Power*, ed. R. Bendix and S. M. Lipset, Glencoe, Illinois, 1953, pp. 372–3, 378, 380, 693.

The well-known conflicts between medium and large property owners which occurred in the United States in the Rooseveltian era also suggest certain new reflexions about the criterion of social class. The owners of medium-sized property whom Roosevelt's legislation was intended to defend against the large property-owners were in fact businessmen or firms disposing of hundreds of thousands of dollars, or even 'small millionaires' threatened by the great concerns and the multi-millionaires. This bitter 'class struggle' which so absorbed American society – and was of great significance for the American social structure – can be presented only within the framework of a scheme of gradation, and not of a scheme of intersecting dichotomies.

There are other reasons why the nineteenth-century conception of social class, in both the liberal and the Marxian interpretations, has lost much of its applicability in the modern world. In situations where changes of social structure are to a greater or lesser degree governed by the decision of the political authorities, we are a long way from social classes as interpreted by Marx, Ward, Veblen or Weber, from classes conceived of as groups determined by their relations to the means of production or, as others would say, by their relations to the market. We are a long way from classes conceived of as groups arising out of the spontaneous activities of individuals or at the most of spontaneously-created class organizations. In situations where the political authorities can overtly and effectively change the class structure; where the privileges that are most essential for social status, including that of a higher share in the national income, are conferred by a decision of the political authorities; where a large part or even the majority of the population is included in a stratification of the type to be found in a bureaucratic hierarchy – the nineteenth-century concept of class becomes more or less an anachronism, and class conflicts give way to other forms of social antagonism.[1]

The planned direction of changes in the social structure and the direct dependence of the economic status of the majority of the population on the state authorities are features that are characteristic of contemporary socialist societies. They are not however confined to these societies. In an interesting paper on *Changes in Patterns of Stratification Attendant on Attainment of Political Inde-*

[1] Cf. the predictions made by Arturo Labriola in the early years of the present century: *Karl Marx – L'économiste – Le socialiste*, Paris 1909, pp. 254, 256, 260.

*pendence*, presented at the Third World Congress of Sociology at Amsterdam in 1956, Dr. S. N. Eisenstadt discussed the role of the political authorities in the formation of social stratification in countries which have just achieved their independence, and in particular in former colonial countries. We can also look for more striking examples. Whereas in his own day, Roosevelt's New Deal was regarded in certain circles as an attack on the old American traditions, today the immense national budget of the United States permits infinitely thorough-going intervention by the political authorities in the economic life of the country and enables them to exert considerable influence on the distribution of the national income and the system of class relations.

In an atmosphere of world tension, the impending danger of war provides a much more convenient cloak than did the cautiously reformist slogans of the New Deal. But the majority of American citizens are becoming accustomed to large-scale activities planned by the central authorities irrespective of any danger of war.[1] Hence comes the talk about the crisis facing political economics, whose laws were formerly rooted in the basic and inevitable tendencies of individual behaviour, but which today faces a dilemma caused by the growing influence of the government as a factor which consciously directs the country's economic life.[1]

Thus the experiences of recent years incline us to formulate the Marxian conception of social class in the form of a law which establishes a functional dependence: the more closely the social system approximates to the ideal type of a free and competitive capitalist society, the more are the classes determined by their relation to the means of production, and the more are human relationships determined by ownership of the means of production.

## Means of Production, Means of Consumption and Means of Compulsion

Economic power over others can be achieved not only through the means of production but also through consumer-goods. This

---

[1] 'And so it comes about' – writes J. M. Clark – 'that we live in a society of organized pressure-groups, of commission-government, public-utility regulation, anti-trust action, farm price supports, social security, supervision of collective bargaining, and the kind of regional planning involved in the Tennessee Valley Authority.' 'America's Changing Capitalism: The Interplay of Politics and Economics[2], in the collective publication, *Freedom and Control in Modern Society*, New York, Van Nostrand Company, 1954, p. 193.

[2] *Ibid.*, p. 204.

was the basis of the economic power of the Principate over the Roman proletariat, which looked to its Caesars not for working tools but for bread and circuses. 'People enslave others with cap, pap and salt' – runs an old Polish proverb (meaning with homage, subsistence and hospitality). But in addition to the means of production and the means of consumption there is also the means of compulsion. The latter was used to acquire in Egypt the corn which assured to the Caesars their economic power over the people of Rome. All three types of relations can be found as motifs in Polish peasant folklore. There the means of compulsion was symbolized by the bailiff's whip and the manor dungeon, the means of production by the land, and the means of consumption by bread. In the folklore of Northern Mazowsze economic power achieved by ownership of consumer goods provided the motif for the tale about the poor peasant who at the behest of his rich brother plucked out his own eyes to get bread for his starving children.

In the society in which Marx's *Das Kapital* and Spencer's *Sociology* were written however, the Caesars did not distribute bread to the great urban populations, while the price of a ticket to the circus was calculated according to the principle of maximum profit.

In our own world the problems of the relation between systems of privilege and systems of human relationships, of the relation between the privilege of controlling the means of production and the privilege of a higher share in the national income, and of the relation between the control over the means of production and the control of the means of compulsion – all these are assuming a new form.

## The Fortunes of Revolutionary Ideologies

A few pages back I referred to the 'apologetic' character of certain interpretations of the class structure: those interpretations which involved a defence of the existing social order against the ideals which we are accustomed to associate with the French Revolution, but which have in reality a much longer history. The need for such apologetics is particularly evident in circumstances in which new privileged classes have actually achieved their new position under the banner of these ideals, which in the changed situation have become a nuisance. The ruling classes or groups regard the consequences derived from these ideals as undesirable and there are two methods of counter-action to which they can resort. One is the overt rejection of the slogans in the name of which power was achieved; the other is the adoption of an appropriate interpretation for both the slogans and the existing social reality. The first method is unlikely to promote social stability, if the victorious ideology has been institutionalized and has bestowed its lustre on the new constitution. It thus represents a positive emotional capital which it would be unwise to abandon. Usually it has an emotional value not only for those who were victorious in its name but also for those who are reared in its traditions later. Maurras, Mussolini or Hitler, who openly rejected the slogans of the *Declaration of the Rights of Man and Citizen*, regarded this act of rejection as a calculated break with the institutions of bourgeois democracy in the name of a new ideology. A century earlier on the other hand, to condemn this declaration was to indicate one's membership of the feudal world which was then facing defeat.

There are considerable analogies to be found within differing social orders for the process whereby the privileged classes verbally appropriate to themselves the principles of the underprivileged classes, and for other phenomena connected with this process. When Christianity became the religion of the ruling classes and the term 'peasant' (*paganus*) became a derogatory name for those who professed the old religion, no attempt was made to remove from the Gospels, the Epistles or the writings of the Fathers of the Church those passages which advocated equality and fraternity. In the year A.D. 313 the Synod, by agreement with the Emperor, condemned those people who appealed to the Gospels when refusing military service (today this would be called a 'left-wing deviation'). Christian doctrine, which had over the centuries been built up into the great system of Aquinas, became the mainstay of the new order, but all the passages of Holy Writ which might prove dangerous for the privileged classes, for the Church hierarchy or for feudal power still retained their binding force. Thus when we view history in simplifying perspective we see Christianity being split into two main streams: the Christianity of the ruling Church, where the teaching of Christ protects the existing order from the dangerous aspirations of those who seek egalitarianism and freedom; and revolutionary Christianity, the Christianity of the mediaeval heretics and the peasant movements, where the teaching of Christ, drawn from the same books sanctioned by the official Church, leads to revolt against the privileged classes, the Church and the State.

In contradistinction to the English bourgeois revolution of the 17th Century, the leaders of the French Revolution no longer sought support in Christian doctrine. They rejected the authority of Holy Writ, and justified on quite different grounds the rights and obligations of the citizen which were associated with the slogans of liberty, equality and fraternity. Once victory had been won and the new order stabilized, the revolutionary slogans became part of the civic catechism in the European and American bourgeois democracies. After being accepted by the two rival camps which were formed on the foundations of the new order, these slogans underwent two kinds of interpretation – in the same way as had happened with the ideological heritage of the early Christian community. One interpretation led towards a new proletarian revolution, while the other reconciled the slogans with the model of a capitalist democracy. In this case too, a common cultural heritage was divided into two opposed streams.

The adaptation of revolutionary slogans to further the stabilization of the new order and the defence of the new privileged class called for other methods in this particular case than in those in which religious doctrine was involved. For the ideology of the bourgeois democracies did not have at its disposal the world after death, into which the realization of the principles of social equality could be transferred without endangering the estate-structure. On the other hand, the new secular ideology was able to make use not only of appropriate interpretations of the existing class structure but also of the doctrine of progress.

The revolutionary stream gave birth to the Marxian system. Later the theories of Marx and Engels, supplemented and brought up to date by the creative effort of Lenin, were, as 'Marxist science', to guide the leaders of the proletarian revolution. And after the victory of that revolution and the establishment of the new order, they became state doctrine and the basis for civic education. In the course of time, Marxism became institutionalized as 'the teachings of Marx, Engels, Lenin and Stalin', which I have even heard referred to on occasion by the symbolic abbreviation

'MELS'. Marxist doctrine, with its powerful, revolutionary dynamism, was, in its new form as a state doctrine, adapted to further the stabilisation of the new regime and to defend the new privileged strata. In the same way as the French revolutionary ideology of the three-fold rights of man or the mediaeval teaching of the Gospels had done, so Marxism, in the period which was to be called the Stalinist period, split into a revolutionary ideology and an official doctrine, petrified in its intellectual content but flexible in its use as an apologetic shield for current policy.

In its official interpretation Christianity justified the discrepancy between the principles of Christ's teaching and reality, on the grounds of the corruption of human nature, which made it impossible for the Kingdom of God to be realized here on earth. For its part, Marxism had at its disposal the theory of dialectical development. By appealing to this, it was possible to justify processes which seemed reactionary from the viewpoint of the aims of Communism, processes in which the gap dividing reality from the postulated future was actually increasing. Using such an interpretation of the dialectical processes it was possible to strive for the attainment of a social order in accordance with the postulate of equality by combating egalitarian trends, even for instance by combating the feeling that emerged in periods of general shortage that the types of ration-cards issued to children should not be dependent on their parents' status. It was possible to strive to achieve a state of freedom by placing increasingly severe restrictions on it.

Apart from the appeal to the dialectic of development to weaken the impression of distance between the existing state of affairs and the ends of Communism, a suitable interpretation of the country's social structure came into use, as I showed in Chapter VII. A convenient interpretation of the principles of equality and liberty was also adapted, as had also been done, though in a different form, by the ideologists of the bourgeois democracies. In both cases, the task was facilitated by the acceptance of certain *a priori* views. In some circumstances these views were regarded as if they were analytical sentences deduced from definitions; in others as synthetic sentences making an assertion about an object known by other means without reference to this particular synthetic sentence. An instance of a thesis of such a dual nature would be the thesis that social classes are only possible in a situation where there exists private ownership of the means of production.

After the words and practices that had served the revolutionary movement had been accepted, they were given a different content or their application was restricted to situations without relevance for everyday life. The sharing of bread and wine continued to bear the name 'communion' when it was transformed into a sacrament given at the altar. On Maundy Thursday the Bishop continued to carry out the ritual of washing beggars' feet, but this action did not involve any risk of lessening the gap which divided him from them nor help to make the relations between the Church dignitaries and the Christian population more democratic. Again, every worker who had the opportunity of making a direct approach to Stalin was able to address him as 'comrade', while a charwoman or porter would be called 'comrade' by those who had unlimited bank-accounts, could shop at special stores and had access to special social services for themselves and their children.

## The Question of Historical Analogies

If this book had been published two or three years earlier than it actually was,[1] the historical analogies which I have just outlined between the fortunes which encounter revolutionary ideologies after their victory would have evoked the most severe charges of being 'a-historical' and 'formalistic' because they compared phenomena arising in different social orders, orders in 'different stages' of historical development. The same charges would also have been made against the earlier chapters of this study, in which I examined certain ways of conceiving the class structure as found in different social orders and in different historical periods.

The demand for the 'historical treatment of phenomena' which was made by social writers and some French historians in the first half of the nineteenth century was, as we know, directed against eighteenth-century conceptions of the unchangeability of human nature; these conceptions ignored the dependence of psychological traits, human needs and the utility of particular institutions on the whole set of concrete historical circumstances. In using historical comparisons, this demand for the 'historical treatment of phenomena' should be regarded as a particular form of the rules

[1] The Polish original came out in 1957.

of scientific procedure, which enjoin caution in drawing conclusions from limited analogies and a clear formulation of the respects in which we are justified in regarding the phenomena under comparison as similar. This demand was used to oppose the application to the field of social phenomena of the method of Cuvier, who reconstructed an entire animal organism from a tooth which had been discovered. If these rules are followed, the increasing profundity and scope of historical and ethnological knowledge, which was not available to the social writers of the eighteenth century nor to various philosophers of history in the nineteenth century, provides a certain protection against unfounded conclusions drawn from historical analogies.

In Marxism the demand for the 'historical treatment of phenomena' has assumed a special significance because of the Marxian theory of development. Owing to the great importance which this theory ascribes to the relations of production for all domains of social life, conclusions derived from comparisons drawn between phenomena occurring in different social orders have had to be regarded as particularly dangerous. It did not however follow from this that phenomena arising in different 'formations' were incomparable. Such a conclusion would have been fatal for the development of knowledge about society and culture. Both Marx and Engels made frequent use of widely-drawn historical analogies: for instance, in discussing the significance of class struggles in the history of culture or in describing social phenomena connected with the exchange of goods. Marx's followers also used such analogies. Kautsky, for instance, even drew a fairly detailed parallel between the groupings in the Hussite camp in Žyzka's day and the parliamentary parties of the nineteenth century. Moreover, all the Marxist or non-Marxist causal explanations of phenomena that occurred in remote eras make use, openly or tacitly, of analogies drawn from the world of today.

The demand for the 'historical treatment of phenomena' was never clearly formulated, and thus in the Stalinist period it easily became a weapon of defence for the existing state of affairs. Whenever institutions or customs in the socialist countries were threatened by dangerous analogies, this demand was transformed into a contention about the incomparability of phenomena taken from different social orders. Inconvenient analogies could be dealt with decisively and without reference to the facts by the use of the term

CONCEPTUAL CONSTRUCTS AND SOCIAL REALITY

'formalism', a term which has, though for quite a different reason, acquired a pejorative flavour in the sphere of art. In conditions in which scholarship was dominated by politics, the demand which we are discussing, the demand which Marx intended to serve the cause of social development and creative thought, became, in the hands of conservative forces, a factor responsible for stagnation or a shield for reaction. To speak of nationalism or of national megalomania in a socialist society was a sin from the viewpoint of this 'Marxist methodology', which did not permit such pejoratively-flavoured concepts from other formations to be applied to phenomena arising in a socialist system. A similar 'methodological' sin was to perceive an element of 'opium for the masses' in certain official propaganda ventures in the countries of socialism. And the same 'methodology' led to the branding as 'formalistic' and 'a-historical' of arguments that there might be a similarity between the arguments put forward in these countries in support of considerable income differentials and the arguments which we have encountered in the history of feudal and capitalist societies.

'You cannot step twice into the same river' – so Heraclitus is reported to have said. Some fail to notice that the river is constantly changing; others do not realize that in certain respects it is always the same river. Both are equally in error. This is equally true of those who do not appreciate the different habits of thought and motivations of action found in people of differing cultures and social orders, and of those who assume in advance that the mind of a man reared in the small hunting communities of the Arctic or Australia or in the matriarchal tribes of Melanesia cannot be compared with that of a contemporary European and that their responses to reality are mutually incomprehensible.[1]

The social scientist must direct his attention equally to the historical specificity of phenomena drawn from different eras and different social systems, and to their comparability in the framework of more comprehensive categories. Our knowledge of the world becomes more profound by following these two paths. The apprehension of similarities and analogous correlations in the most remote fields and the more widely differing circumstances has frequently been the source of important discoveries in the history of knowledge.

[1] Cf. L. Levy-Brühl: *Les fonctions mentales dans les societés inférieures*, Paris, 1909.

This is more than a matter of theory – particularly in the sphere of our problems. Once it was thought that the nationalization of the means of production would automatically result in a fundamental change in human relations. After the experience of recent decades we know that this does not necessarily happen: that the principle 'social existence determines consciousness' does not entitle us to draw such simple conclusions, because 'social existence' is not a simple matter. If the nationalization of the major means of production is a necessary condition for the sort of system of human relations towards which the pioneers of Communism were striving, it is still not a sufficient condition. If one embarks on a fundamental reconstruction, then it is of the utmost importance to have one's eyes open to the great variety of relationships between phenomena and the great variety of their similarities, and to distinguish between what is new and what is simply the same thing in a new guise. This consideration was one of the motives which led me to study the problem of class structure on a broad comparative basis.

One of the important consequences of the events which took place in Poland in 1956, and above all the events of the so-called Polish October, was the destruction of the official myths which concealed our reality. Since then wide possibilities have opened up for deliberate and direct endeavours to form a socialist culture; the scholar should not overlook, amongst the tasks awaiting him, the duty of watching out for the social consequences of habits of thought left to us by the past. I am thinking here not only of the relics of capitalist culture but of thought-patterns of more recent origin, dating from the times of the grim myth with which those who were reconciled to the existing state of affairs salved their consciences: the myth of historical necessity as revealed to those who wield power.

# INDEX

Abel, *see* Cain
Abramowski, Edward, viii
Agrippa, *see* Menenius Agrippa
Alembert, d', 98, 122
Ambrosius, 169
America, pre-Revolutionary, 43; *see also* United States
America, Latin, 45, 48, 52
American Creed, the, 36, 105, 107, 109, 110, 113, 114, 114–15, 115–16, 153
American railway trains, *see* classes in
American sociology, *see* sociology
antagonistic relations in society, 30, 34, 184; *see also* class antagonism
Antal, F., 64
Aquinas, St Thomas, 14, 64, 187
Archer, William, 105, 107
Aristotle, 12, 14, 28, 29, 39–40, 41, 42, 51, 58, 90, 149, 172–3
Assorodobraj, N., 27 n., 126 n.
asymmetrical relations between social classes, 31, 41, 57, 64, 87, 90, 147; *see also* dependence
atomic energy, 3; a civilization of social planning and, 181
Augustine, St, 19, 29, 40, 180

Babeuf, Gracchus, 14, 26, 33, 37, 70, 86, 123, 147, 174
Ball, John, 25 n.
Baudelaire, Charles, 22
Beals, R. C., 48, 52
Beard, C. and M., 36 n.
bees and drones, 25–28
Bell, D., 61 n.
Bernard, Jessie, 100 n.
Bierut, President, 112
*bogaty* ('rich'), etymology of the word, 20
Bryce, J., 158, 173
Bucharin, N., 72, 78 n.
Bunche, Ralph, 105

Cain and Abel, 20, 21, 22
Cantril, H., 45 n., 103
capital and labour, Marx's clarification of the relations between, 71
capitalism, 1, 41; classical period of, 126–7, 181
capitalist class, *see* class
capitalist society: consequences of for European thought, 181; development of not in accordance with Marxian predictions, 104, 181, 182; ideal type of, 62; Marxian predictions concerning, 75, 96; Marxian scheme of class structure an analysis of, 76, 83; Marxist analysis applied by Soviet Union to, 116; non-capitalist relations of production in, 83; post-capitalistic societies, 128
caste, relation between class and, 102, 108–09, 130–1
caste systems, 32, 51, 63–65, 129–30, 140, 154; economic classes in, 65–68
castes, 19–20, 22, 32, 63 ff., 140; separation of in U.S.A., 108–09
Centers, R., 44 n., 45, 46 n., 49, 54, 56, 101, 103–04, 106 n., 108, 162
Ceylon, 137 n.
'Chevroletariat', 137
China, ancient, 42
Christianity: dichotomic scheme in, 22–23; of the Church, and revolutionary, 187–8, 189, 190
Church, Catholic, 23 n.
Church Fathers, 12, 29, 180, 187
Clark, J. M., 185 n.
class, emotional charge connected with the word, 167
'class': and 'estate', relation between the terms, 122, 124–5, 128, 162; 'order' as term for, 59, 123, 126, 162; use of term in sense of 'social class', 122, 124

ruling groups:—*continued*
  but useful against others, 116–17;
  their tendency to efface 'class' nature
  of social structure, 89, 154
Russia, *see* Soviet Union
Russian emigré intellectuals, 116 f.
Ryan, B., 137 n.

Saint-Simon, 14, 27, 33, 50, 123–4, 174
Savary, 43
schemes of class and social structure, *see*
  dichotomic, functional, gradation,
  Marxian, trichotomous
Schumpeter, J., 136 n., 148, 157 n.
semantic conventions, viewpoints concerning, 158–61
serfs, 19, 21
Servius Tullus, 93
Shelley's 'Song to the Men of England',
  26–27, 150, 174
Sieyès, Abbé, 36–37, 123
Sjoberg, C., 103 n., 115
Skarga, Peter, 58–59
slavery, 19, 28–30, 34
Smith, Adam: his theory of social
  classes, 14, 59–69, 62, 79, 80, 83, 84,
  87, 90, 111, 113, 123, 147, 149 n., 150,
  151, 162
'social', terms deprived of spatial
  connotation by the adjective, 10
social class, classes, *see* class, social, *and*
  classes, social
social consciousness: how the term is
  here used, 6; and the test of reality,
  38; conceptions of social structure in,
  6–7, 66; reflection of the class system
  in, 19, 105; shaped by the Marxian
  system, 69, 181; studies of social
  structure concerned with, 56; synthetic evaluations as an expression of,
  55
social distance, 7, 10, 35, 51, 136–8,
  140; *see also* class boundaries
social ecology, 10
social facts, views of class structure as,
  12
social inequalities, 29, 94–95, 99, 107,
  140; abolition of, 154; *see also*
  dichotomic scheme, *amd* classlessness,
  non-egalitarian
social isolation, *see* social distance
social mobility, 10, 93, 94, 110, 154
social morphology, 10

social order, defence of the existing, 27,
  29, 90–92, 178–9, 186–90
social problems, vii, viii, 5–6
social reality and conceptual constructs,
  2 ff., 5, 28, 30, 32, 33, 38, 104, 115–16;
  121–93 *passim*
social sciences: handicap to the development of the, 3–4; need for new concepts and methods in the, 4, and for
  conceptual clarification, 9; propaganda functions of the, 116; *see also*
  sociology
social status in a scheme of gradation,
  factors determining, 47–49; counterbalancing of, 52; consistency in, 53
social status continuum, *see* continuum
social stratification, 7, 19–20, 29, 44,
  45, 49, 52, 102, 106; *see also* class
  structure, classes, social, gradation
'social stratum', use of the term, 45, 54,
  73, 162
social structure:
  how the term is here used, 5
  actual, contrasted with dominant
    relations in the, 83
  classes in the, exhaustive or nonexhaustive division of, 141–3; *see*
    *also* class society, class structure,
    *and* classlessness, non-egalitarian
  concept of, 10–11; Marxian synthesis
    of conceptions of, 70; several ways
    of conceiving, in the works of
    Marx and Engels, 86
  images of, importance of, 6–7;
    complication of the image of the,
    33
  interpretations of: comparison of
    American and Soviet, 100–18
    (American views, 101–10; Soviet
    views, 110–13; comparison, 113–18);
    similar interpretations in mutually
    opposed systems, 101, 114–15
  metaphors used in describing, 7–9
  schemes of: a three-term scheme, 31,
    32–33 (*see also* dichotomic, functional, gradation, Marxian, trichotomous); typology of, 145–55;
    correlation of same with typology
    of actual structures, 172–5; choice
    of viewpoint dictated by nature of
    problem studied or by a particular
    belief about reality, 175–7
  *see also* spatial structure